TEACH YOU

op

opera

Susan Sutherland

TEACH YOURSELF BOOKS

For UK order queries: please contact Bookpoint Ltd, 39 Milton Park, Abingdon, Oxon OX14 4TD. Telephone: (44) 01235 400414, Fax: (44) 01235 400454. Lines are open from 9.00 – 6.00, Monday to Saturday, with a 24 hour message answering service. Email address: orders@bookpoint.co.uk

For U.S.A. & Canada order queries: please contact/Contemporary Publishing, 4255 West Touhy Avenue, Lincolnwood, Illinois 60646 – 1975 U.S.A. Telephone: (847) 679 5500, Fax: (847) 679 2494.

Long-renowned as the authoritative source for self-guided learning – with more than 30 million copies sold worldwide – the *Teach Yourself* series includes over 200 titles in the fields of languages, crafts, hobbies, sports, and other leisure activities.

British Library Cataloguing in Publication Data
A catalogue record for this title is available from The British Library

Library of Congress Catalog Card Number: 96-72382

First published in UK 1997 by Hodder Headline Plc, 338 Euston Road, London NW1 3BH.

First published in US 1997 by NTC/Contemporary Publishing, 4255 West Touhy Avenue, Lincolnwood (Chicago), Illinois 60646 – 1975 U.S.A.

The 'Teach Yourself' name and logo are registered trade marks of Hodder & Stoughton Ltd.

Copyright © 1997 Susan Sutherland

Typeset by Transet Limited, Coventry, England.
Printed in Great Britain for Hodder & Stoughton Educational, a division of Hodder Headline Plc, 338 Euston Road, London NW1 3BH by Cox & Wyman Ltd, Reading, Berkshire.

Impression number	14	13	12	11	10	9	8	7	6	5	4
Year		2003	2002	2001	2000	1999	1998				

Acknowledgements

When I was a little girl my favourite songs were, *The Teddy Bears Picnic, Rock around the Clock* and *Celeste Aida.* For this broad acceptance of what constitutes a good tune, I thank my mother for ensuring that my young life was filled with all types of music.

My singing teachers at the Royal College of Music, the late Frederic Cox CBE and Sylvia Jacobs, encouraged a deeper study of opera, fostering an interest that has never waned.

Stephen Wilkinson MBE, then Director of the BBC Northern Singers, broadened my horizons, giving me the opportunity to sing works 'off the beaten track', both contemporary and early. Tony Rooley, visting tutor at the music department of the University of York, opened my mind to the magical intricacies of 'early opera'. My husband gave me the confidence to put my thoughts into words, my children Sara, James and Leonie gave me the challenge of discovering which bit of work they had wiped off the computer and my friends gave me tolerance when I turned myself into a hermit as the deadline approached.

All my friends at Hodder & Stoughton have given me nothing but encouragement and support throughout and special thanks must go to Joanne Osborn, Sarah Mitchell, Sue Hart and Myra Bennett.

For my mother, Elizabeth Greenwood:
'thank you for the music...'

CONTENTS

INTRODUCTION

❢ Opera is – a pompous piece of folly ❢
Charles de Marguetel de Saint-Denis,
Seigneur de Saint-Evremond, 1610–1703

This seventeenth-century observation has bedevilled opera throughout its history, deterring many from discovering that opera can be relevant, accessible and vastly entertaining. *Teach Yourself Opera* introduces you to a selection of the best and offers you an insight into their background, as well as the life and times of their composers.

A brief and entertaining history of opera will guide you through the various developments, allowing you to increase your knowledge, both through eyewitness accounts and historical facts, and a table allows you to see at a glance where a particular opera belongs in the historical sense. There is a full explanation of the many ingredients that go into the creation of an opera, together with plot outlines to explain the story. Special highlights are brought to your attention and various ways to get the most out of an opera are explored.

This is not intended to be either an exhaustive, or an exhausting study, but a tasty appetizer that leads you confidently into the world of opera.

The real adventure begins in Part Three when specific works are featured. You may discover some that are new to you, or find that you can listen to familiar works with a keener understanding. This section begins with *The Magic Flute* by Mozart, the biggest success for this composer in his lifetime. There's glorious music of course and some of the most exciting vocal pyrotechnics to be found in any opera.

Difficult to top? Certainly. But not impossible to follow as Puccini proves with his opera, *La Bohème*.

Experience the sensational scoring of Mimi's death scene and the orgasmic culmination of Musetta's 'Waltz song'. *La Bohème* is so tightly written, its pace compares with the best contemporary film script.

Opera is an intense experience. All of life's emotions packed into a tight schedule, with a style of singing that demands total dedication and supreme effort from the performers. To add to this potent mix, dramas within the plot have sometimes been matched, or even surpassed by real-life dramas. For where you find genius, giant egos, great fame and fabulous wealth, scandal, gossip and intrigue cannot be far behind.

No book on opera could possibly be complete without some mention of these and *Teach Yourself Opera* aims not to disappoint!

HOW TO USE
THIS BOOK

A trip to the opera can be an expensive option, as can the purchase of tapes and CDs, but the more you know, the less likely you are to make a mistake. Part One of this book introduces you to the different individuals who are involved in opera, as well as explaining some of the terms you are likely to come across. To supplement this, there is a full glossary at the end of the book, covering many other words and phrases associated with opera. The first section ends with suggestions of just a few of the many exciting places for you to visit.

In Part Two you will find the history of opera. Don't be put off at the end of this section by the table and chronological list of a variety of composers with some of their significant works. These are here so that you can refer back, dip into, and generally get a sense of perspective over the 300 years or more of opera's existence. You may also find these useful in helping you to identify particular areas that you would like to go into more deeply at some other time. The text that follows these lists is full of interesting titbits, along with all the facts and figures, so hopefully you will find plenty to amuse and entertain you as you learn more about opera.

Part Three of the book is perhaps the most exciting, because here you will be able to examine some of the most popular operas more closely. These works have not earned their place in opera's 'top ten' for nothing and I feel confident that you will gain as much pleasure from reading about and listening to them, as I have from writing about them.

At the end of each main section there is a short list of self-test questions. You are in charge and can choose to learn as much, or as little as you like. If you are planning a visit to the opera with friends, these questions and answers provide you with some basic topics of conversation for each operatic era and style. Live performances may be mediocre, should be superb, but can be excruciatingly bad – speak your mind and don't be put off for ever if your first experience falls into the excruciating category!

An opera is rather like a beautiful painting. Each time you return, you should find something new to enjoy, but just like a painting, opera is also controversial. Some you may hate, some you will love and some may leave you stone cold. Give yourself time to decide what's right for you, it might be the easily digested romance of Puccini, the powerful drama of Verdi or the mystical epics of Wagner. Some music is right for different stages in your life, or right for the moment. I hope that after this brief introduction you will feel moved to experiment and delve into the rich catalogue of music that lies beyond these few suggestions.

Good hunting and good listening to you all.

Susan Sutherland, 1997

Part One

OVERTURE AND BEGINNERS

AN INTRODUCTION TO OPERA

1
WHAT TO EXPECT

The overture

In the earliest operas, a brief musical flourish might be all that was required to announce the start of the proceedings. The idea of an overture, or opening piece, to introduce tunes or motifs that would reoccur as the drama unfolded, was established by the eighteenth century. This longer overture was seen as a useful device for admitting latecomers, hushing talkers and preparing the audience for the entertainment to come. The approach by composers through the ages to the overture, or lack of one, is as individual as their music. An overture by Rossini might bear no relation whatever to the music to follow, but left the audience in no doubt that the show was about to begin and that they were in for a double helping of the style of entertainment they anticipated. Wagner preferred to prepare his audience psychologically, whilst Verdi and Puccini, amongst others, sometimes raised the curtain directly on the drama. In this case, the music evolves from, and enhances the action on-stage. Comparisons could be drawn to a modern film score, except that the plot is carried forward by song and recitative, rather than speech.

Conductor

Why do the performers and the orchestra need a conductor, since they seem to be ignoring him or her completely?

It's true to say that the orchestra and singers may sometimes be on autopilot for part of a performance, but some cues and certain changes of pace rely on one individual to bring all the elements of music together harmoniously. A good conductor, like any good accompanist, is also sensitive to the immediate needs of all the performers.

The ability to nurse along, or cover for anyone who is not working up to par, and a keen sense of theatrical, as well as musical timing are particular abilities required by an opera conductor. More than this, each conductor puts a unique stamp upon a work. This evolves both through the effect of the conductor's personality and through the research and study undertaken before arriving at a particular interpretation of the music. Works from the seventeenth and eighteenth century would have been conducted, or directed, largely from the keyboard. As the orchestra grew in size, the leader of the violins took increasing responsibility for keeping the musicians together and would sometimes tap out the beat to the distraction of the audience.

The seventeenth-century French composer of Italian birth, Jean-Baptiste Lully, died from gangrene of the foot, after accidentally hitting himself with the big stick he used to beat time on the floor . . . Some music lovers might say, serve him right, but in France, matters were complicated by the use of a large chorus and so the need for some more distinct control had become imperative. It took a little time for the best method to be established and for a while, the director of proceedings really did stand beside the orchestra, punching the ground with a large staff. With this history, it's not surprising that the role of the modern conductor came about. At last there was a true musical director whose sole purpose was to inspire, direct and co-ordinate the musical outpourings, both on-stage and in the orchestra pit.

A piece of rolled-up manuscript was sometimes used as an aid for performers who might be relying on peripheral vision, rather than being able at any precise moment to stare directly at the conductor. Later still, the baton, or stick was used, enabling singers and musicians to catch sight even more easily of the conductor's arm movement.

The counter tenor voice fell out of favour in the eighteenth and nine-teenth centuries, but was revived in the twentieth century by the English counter-tenor, Alfred Deller. Roles for this voice type include: Oberon (*A Midsummer Night's Dream*; Britten), Akhnaten (*Akhnaten*; Philip Glass).

Castrato

(*lit.* castrated.) The barbaric custom of castrating young boys before their voices broke prevented thickening of the vocal chords, so that the voice remained agile and similar in range to a female voice, whilst strengthening to full maturity like any other aspect of the adoles-cent's body.

Although in the sixteenth century these singers were mainly employed for religious purposes, the emergence of opera in the seven-teenth century, provided them with fresh opportunities to show off their considerable talents. Forming an exclusive clique within the singing fraternity, on the one hand *castrati* were revered for their ability as performers, whilst on the other, vanity and affected mannerisms made some of them figures of fun.

By the eighteenth century, *castrati* were an intrinsic part of operatic culture, yet they remained separate within this world, victims of the mixed blessing bestowed by their difference. However, the exceptional technique of the greatest of these singers was renowned throughout the musical world. In the nineteenth century, the rise of *opera verismo*, with its 'true to life' ethos, heralded the decline of this voice type. The last known castrato, (who did not sing in opera), was Alessandro Moreschisi who died in 1922, aged 64.

Baritone

Generally having a deeper tone than a tenor voice, the baritone voice began to require separate categorisation from the bass voice in eighteenth-century opera, due to the distinct character of roles being created by composers such as Mozart. The term *baritonan* had been used as early as the fifteenth century, denoting a deep-sounding male voice, but right up to the eighteenth century most parts written for a deep male voice were referred to as **bass**. Famous baritone roles include: Papageno (*The Magic Flute*; Mozart), Figaro (*The Barber of Seville*; Rossini), The Count (*The Marriage of Figaro*; Mozart), Escamillo (*Carmen*; Bizet).

Bass

The lowest category of male voice, the bass is generally regarded as falling into three main types; the bass-baritone, the buffo bass and the basso-profundo.

- **Bass-baritone**   As the name suggests a male voice that has something of the gravitas and power of the bass, combined with the fluidity and range of the baritone. Famous bass-baritone roles include: Wotan (*Der Ring des Nibelungen*; Wagner), Hans Sachs (*Der Meistersinger von Nürnberg*; Wagner).
- **Buffo-bass**   Character roles, requiring a singer with personality able to carry off a wide range of expression including comedy; e.g. Leporello (*Don Giovanni*; Mozart), Bartolo (*The Marriage of Figaro*; Mozart).
- **Basso-profondo**   This, the deepest of the male voice types, provides many of the most solemn and portentous moments in an opera. e.g. Sarastro (*The Magic Flute*; Mozart), Oroveso (*Norma*; Bellini).

⎯⎯ Some outstanding singers ⎯⎯

Sixteenth century

Marchetto Cara   Commentary by Baldassare Castiglione, writing in 1561: 'and no less does our Marchetto Cara move in his singing, but with a more soft harmony, that by a delectable way and full of mourning sweetness, maketh tender and pierceth the mind, and sweetly imprinteth in it a passion of great delight'.

Seventeenth century

Giulio Caccini (1545–1618)   An outstanding tenor, who was to become a notable composer and trail-blazing teacher of the bel canto style of singing.

Ladies of Ferrara (c. 1570s)   A trio of lady singers, famed throughout Europe for their beautiful, expressive singing and unprecedented technique. The court at Ferrara was renowned for the excellence of its music.

Adriana Basile (1580–1640)   Monteverdi declared this Italian contralto to be the finest singer of her time.

Eighteenth century

Carlo Broschi 'Farinelli' (1705–82)   The most famous of all castrati, this Italian singer, known as Farinelli, was noted, in the early years of his career, for his astonishing displays of vocal agility and technique. He matured into a performer of great skill and sensitivity, and expert historical opinion leads to the conclusion that he was one of the greatest singers of all time. Reputed to be a cultured and congenial man, he was a friend of the librettist, Metastasio, established an Italian Opera in Madrid and later became a diplomat, eventually retiring on a large pension to live in considerable style in Bologna.

Josepha (c. 1758–1819) *and Aloysia Weber* (c. 1759–1839)   Two of the three sisters of Mozart's wife, Constanze. Mozart wrote the part of The Queen of the Night for Josepha and fell in love with Aloysia, who did not share his passion. Of Aloysia, he wrote, she had 'a pure, lovely voice' and was capable of 'superb cantabile singing'. He wrote several arias for Aloysia and she created the role of Donna Anna, in the first performance in Vienna of *Don Giovanni*.

Nancy Storace (1765–1817)   This English singer created the role of Susannah in Mozart's opera, *The Marriage of Figaro*. At her debut, in a minor role in Florence at the age of 15, she outsang the famous castrato Marchesi, and was promptly invited to leave the production. She met Mozart in Vienna, where her gift for comedy and lovely voice made her a great favourite.

Nineteenth century

Luigi Lablache (1794–1858)   A singer of prodigious talent, this famous bass thrilled audiences as much with his dramatic qualities as with his voice. Comedy, tragedy and all stops between were projected effortlessly by this half-Irish, half-French singer. Schubert dedicated three songs to Lablache, Wagner was an admirer, as were several monarchs, including Queen Victoria, to whom he gave singing lessons. Amongst others, he created the role of Don Pasquale in Donizetti's opera of the same name and Lord Walton in the opera *I Puritani* by Bellini.

Giuditta Pasta (1797–1865)   One of the first divas, Pasta owed much of her success to relentless study. Unwisely agreeing some time after her official retirement, to one final performance, Pasta provided a tragic spectacle. A fellow artiste, Madam Viardot commented tearfully to a friend, 'you are right! It is like – a wreck of a picture, but the wreck of the greatest picture in the world!'

Maria Malibran (1808–36)   A brief, but passionate life; the Belgian scholar and composer, Francois-Joseph Fetis, declared this Spanish mezzo-soprano to be, 'the most astonishing singer of the century'. Exceptionally charismatic and an impassioned interpreter of any role she undertook, Madame Malibran could count amongst her admirers, Verdi, Chopin, Hans Anderson, Bellini, Paganini and Donizetti, and Legouve said of her, 'she is one of those artists who cause art to advance, because they are always seeking.' Her sister was Pauline Viardot, another renowned mezzo-soprano. Both sisters received their initial vocal training from their father, Manuel Garcia, a famous singer and celebrated teacher, for whom Rossini wrote the part of Count Almaviva.

Jenny Lind (1820–87)   Possessing a precocious talent, this Swedish soprano became known as the 'Swedish Nightingale'. By the age of 21, she had sung many of the most vocally demanding leading roles in her home country and her voice had begun to suffer the consequences of undertaking too much too soon. A period of retraining in Paris led fortunately to the revival of her vocal powers and she went on to become an international celebrity. Renowned for her extraordinary breath control and the extreme brilliance and purity of her upper register, Jenny Lind excelled in roles requiring pathos and innocence.

Adelina Patti (1843–1919)   The daughter of renowned singers, whose mother was said to have sung the role of Norma the night before she was born, this Italian singer was born in Madrid and studied in New York, where she made her debut. Among her many admirers was Verdi, who declared himself to be entranced by the extraordinary sweetness and flexibility of her voice, together with her convincing dramatic presence. Adored by the public, Adelina Patti was able to demand huge fees, exemption from rehearsals, approval over publicity and control over any other matter concerning herself. She amassed a jewel collection of such value that she was forced to travel with her own guards. Her elder sisters, Amalia and Carlotta, were also fine singers and some were of the opinion that Carlotta was as good as Adelina. Unfortunately, Carlotta was lame and her singing was confined to the concert, rather than the operatic stage.

Twentieth century

Dame Nellie Melba (1861–1931) '*I* am *Melba*', this Australian diva would proclaim when her authority was challenged. On her dressing-room door, to which only she held the key, was a notice – 'Melba. Silence! Silence!' Even the great Caruso had to be content with a fee of £399, to Dame Nellie's £400, for she had to be seen to earn more. If this gives a clue as to the character of this great singer, it is still only part of the story. A blunt speaker, Nellie Melba was no snob. Whilst stage hands in Sydney were still reeling from an unexpected visit by the famous lady, she treated them to an impromptu concert and then took her bow as humbly as on any glittering first night.

This down-to-earth, take me, or leave me attitude, combined with a prodigious talent, earned Dame Nellie the respect of everyone, but her charm did not extend to those unfortunate enough to find themselves in the position of her employer.

Enrico Caruso (1873–1921) An Italian tenor of many exceptional qualities, Enrico Caruso became a legend within his lifetime, thanks to the advent of mass communication. His remarkable voice was only part of the picture, because Caruso possessed artistry beyond the usual. His acting skills were enhanced by his expertise with stage make-up, and his breath control and musical phrasing were exemplary. He countered Melba's high-handed attitude with a number of practical jokes, including handing her a hot sausage in the middle of 'your tiny hand is frozen', and on another occasion, placing a chamber pot under her 'death bed'. The number and variety of roles in which he excelled was enormous. At the Metropolitan Opera House in New York alone, he gave 600 performances between 1903 and 1920. Fortunately, there are recordings available and with the aid of digital enhancement it is possible to appreciate something of the gifts of this outstanding singer.

Feodor Chaliapin (1873–1938) A self-taught Russian bass of humble origins, in his most famous role, that of Boris Godunov in the opera of the same name, Chaliapin was instrumental in putting Mussorgsky on the operatic map. In a letter to Chaliapin, Maxim Gorky wrote, 'You are to music what Tolstoy is to literature'. At Chaliapin's funeral in Paris which was attended by thousands of Russians, one of them, Prince Zeretelli, commented, 'there will be no other like him . . . he was Russia.'

Beniamino Gigli (1890–1957) This Italian tenor was regarded as Caruso's successor. Never noted for his acting ability, his exquisite voice more than compensated for any dramatic shortfalls. Adored by the public, Gigli's superb technique served him well, allowing him to pursue his career well into his sixties.

Kirsten Flagstad (1895–1962) Up to 1933, this Norwegian singer had been known only in her own country. On the point of retirement, she was invited to sing at Bayreuth. The rest, as they say, is history. She went on to become possibly the greatest Wagnerian soprano of all time.

Jussi Björling (1911–60) This Swedish lyric tenor was perhaps the Carreras of his generation. His musicianship, thrilling voice and thoughtful character portrayals brought him huge and well-deserved success.

Kathleen Ferrier (1912–53) An exceptional English contralto, Kathleen Ferrier's early death came just at the moment her career blossomed. A tragic loss to the operatic world, she was known as much for her warm, down-to-earth manner, as for her unusually rich and beautiful voice. She created the part of Lucrezia, in Britten's opera, *The Rape of Lucrezia* and is perhaps best remembered singing Orfeo, in Gluck's opera, *Orfeo ed Euridice*.

Tito Gobbi (1913–84) This Italian baritone had such a facility for acting, he could have been termed a 'singing actor', if his voice hadn't been quite so exceptional. His voice was never a huge instrument, but Gobbi nevertheless used its melifluous quality with intelligence. With great charisma and popular both on and off the stage, Tito Gobbi is remembered as one of opera's brightest stars.

Boris Christoff (1914–93) A Bulgarian bass who, because of his imposing presence and skillful acting, together with his impressive voice, was referred to as Chaliapin's successor.

Birgit Nilsson (b. 1918) An outstanding Wagnerian soprano, this Swedish singer combined an imposing stage presence with beauty and a voice that was effortless, incredibly powerful, yet capable of the greatest subtlety.

Guiseppe di Stefano (b. 1921) In his early career, this singer had the most exciting voice. His partnership with Callas, in particular, was electrifying. Sadly, his voice failed early, cutting short what had been a brief, but glorious career.

Geraint Evans (1922–92)   Sir Geraint Evans was a Welsh baritone of particular warmth and charisma. His acting skills and the excellence of his diction in particular, set him apart from his peers. Geraint Evans is also remembered for his opera productions, both in Britain and the United States.

Renata Tebaldi (b. 1922)   Definitely a singer, rather than an actress, this Italian soprano possessed an extremely fine voice which she could use with great subtlety and power when required. Rivalling Callas, in some people's eyes, Tebaldi certainly had the voice, but the extra qualities, necessary to match the allure of Callas, were missing.

Maria Callas (1923–77)   With a voice of crystal clarity in her youth, Maria Callas possessed the illusive star quality in bucketfuls. More than mere personality, or assertiveness, she possessed a power to move that transcended technique, or bald facts like whether or not a note was a little harsh, or not perfectly in tune. The voice had an unusual and unique timbre that carried emotion like an arrow to the heart. American born, Mary Kalogeropoulou, or Maria Callas, as she was to become, moved to Greece when she was 14, trained there and sang Tosca in Athens at the age of 19. Extremely musical, highly intelligent and a fine actress, who could have chosen the straight theatre for her career, Maria Callas is one of the greatest performers ever to have graced the operatic stage.

Victoria de Los Angeles (b. 1923)   Lyrical and charming, both on the concert and operatic stage, this Spanish soprano has given much pleasure with her affecting interpretations and easy, clear-toned voice.

Carlo Bergonzi (b. 1924)   Starting out as a baritone, the Italian singer Carlo Bergonzi trained up to a tenor. He was particularly popular at the Metropolitan Opera House in New York, where he sang regularly for over 30 years. Never a huge voice, but one that was always delivered beautifully and accurately.

Dietrich Fischer-Dieskau (b. 1925)   Also famed for his masterly interpretation of *Lieder*, or Romantic art song, this German baritone's secure technique and commanding stage presence, together with his sensitive delivery of words, brought him international recognition.

John Vickers (b. 1926)   One of the great dramatic singers of the twentieth century, this Canadian tenor was much in demand for Wagnerian, and other meaty roles. A big man with a stage presence to match, John Vickers combined successfully expressive qualities with a large, but melifluous voice.

Joan Sutherland (b. 1926)   *La Stupenda*, as this Australian soprano became known, excelled in the art of bel canto singing. With a warm voice that mirrored her personality, Dame Joan Sutherland's mastery of the most intricate embellishments and unforced, high-ranging voice, earned her enormous success and immense popularity. Sacrificing all in the name of music meant that diction was occasionally thrown to the wind, but the delight of hearing this lady sing far outweighed such quibbles. Joan Sutherland was coached by her husband and musical director, Richard Bonynge, and her equal has yet to make an appearance.

Janet Baker (b. 1933)   A mellow, yet vibrant and very beautiful tone marks out this English mezzo-soprano as one of the great voices of the twentieth century. Dame Janet Baker excelled in English music, although her career was wide ranging, allowing her to demonstrate her mastery in a variety of dramatic roles from Monteverdi to Britten.

Montserrat Caballé (b. 1933)   One of the most highly prized skills of bel canto singing, is the *messa di voce*, which means literally, placing of the voice. The voice is controlled so that it swells, then diminishes to the finest sound on a single note. Montserrat Caballé excelled in this affecting technique and was able to employ it in many of the leading roles which she undertook throughout her international career. One of the great Spanish sopranos, her recording, *Barcelona*, with the singer Freddie Mercury, became a huge chart success in 1992.

Marilyn Horne (b. 1934)   Possessing a strong and versatile instrument, this American mezzo-soprano has a huge range and an immaculate technique. She dubbed the voice of Dorothy Dandridge in the 1954 film of *Carmen Jones*, and amongst many outstanding performances, her recording partnership with Joan Sutherland, in Bellini's opera, *Norma*, is unforgettable.

Sherrill Milnes (b. 1935)   This American baritone is perhaps best known for his Verdian roles. A strong top and a warm tone throughout the instrument, made his singing a delight.

Teresa Berganza (b. 1935)   One of the most sought-after mezzo-sopranos of her day, this world-class Spanish singer possessed a powerful stage presence as well as a beautiful and technically brilliant voice.

Luciano Pavarotti (b. 1935) *The* tenor voice of the century. It would be a mistake to allow the fact of this singer's vast commercial success to cloud the issue. Possessing an instrument of the greatest beauty, power and technical assurance, Pavarotti is also a master of giving his public what they want. This might be *'con belto'* for some of the time, but he is capable of much more. Singing from the heart and with total commitment, he has brought music into the lives of vast numbers of people; a gift not given to many.

Placido Domingo (b. 1941) Born in Spain, Placido Domingo moved to Mexico when he was nine, and it was in this country that he began his career as a baritone. He sang his first major tenor role in 1961, in Dallas, USA. A charismatic stage presence combined with a beautiful and technically assured voice make him one of the leading tenors of his generation. One of the famous Three Tenors, just as with Pavarotti, it would be a mistake to allow all the hullabaloo of commercial success to mask the exceptional quality of this outstanding performer.

Kiri Te Kanawa (b. 1944) A beautiful singer from New Zealand, with a ravishing lyric soprano voice, Dame Kiri Te Kanawa is one of the closest to Diva status of female singers today. The lack of Callas-like stage presence and charisma, are perhaps the only ingredients missing in an otherwise perfect package.

Jessye Norman (b. 1945) A sensational and individual soprano voice, combined with an imposing presence, great warmth, wit and intelligence, are the gifts to relish of this American singer. With a vast repertoire of roles to choose from, no recording collection should be without at least one example of this great lady's work.

José Carreras (b. 1946) A Spanish lyric tenor of the greatest quality, José Carreras is a master of phrasing and subtlety. Having contracted leukaemia in 1987, he made a miraculous recovery, returning to sing at Covent Garden in 1991. One of the Three Tenors, what José Carreras may lack in sheer volume, he more than makes up for with his luscious tone quality and instinctive musicianship. As with the other two members of the Three Tenors, it would be a mistake to allow the fact of this singer's commercial success, to distract from his outstanding artistic qualities.

Bryn Terfel (b. 1965) Winning the *lieder* prize in 1989 at the Cardiff Singer of the Year competition, brought this talented young bass-baritone to the attention of the world. Failing to win the main singing prize was a quirk of fate that fortunately has not hindered him.

Gaining a wealth of experience on-stage in the major houses of the world, rather than leaping straight into the recording studio, has enriched his performances enormously. His recent recording of music by Rodgers and Hammerstein, demonstrates the breadth of his talent, which runs the gamut from Wagner to Broadway.

You may be tempted to wonder why it should be that apart from the Three Tenors, many of today's singers lack the drawing power and charisma of say, Maria Callas, Joan Sutherland, or Enrico Caruso. Even more telling, when you look through lists of recommended recordings in magazines, or visit your local classical record shop seeking advice you are quite likely to find that recommendations favour recordings made 20, or even 30 years ago.

Great voices certainly do exist, but perhaps the rush from conservatoire to recording studio is denying some young singers the stage experience they need to hone timing, dramatic presence and the acting skills necessary for them to develop a fully rounded artistic persona.

The director

Up to the nineteenth century, the overall design of an opera, interpretation of the various parts and required movements for each individual, were guided by the principal organisers of the project. This might be the music director of a particular court, or theatre, one or more of the principal performers, or an impresario, such as Schikaneder. By the nineteenth century, stage managers took on the responsibility, and yet a further refinement occurred with the advent of composers such as Verdi and Wagner, who viewed their compositions as total concepts, in both the visual and aural sense. As the role of production director grew in significance, it attracted artistic individuals who could put their own stamp on a particular opera. In the twentieth century the role of director became ever more prominent with much celebrity being attached to the most successful. Some twentieth-century directors have abused their powers, delivering up travesties of original works, but the public is neither gullible, nor prepared to fund ego trips of this sort and the wilder excesses are increasingly giving way to preferred styles of performance for singers, musicians and public alike.

Librettist

Libretto means literally 'little book'. In the early days of opera, these books of words were published separately and would begin with a preface addressed to the librettist's patron. This allowed the writer a clear way of presenting his work and demonstrated to his patron that his investment was both valued and well spent. This would be followed by an address to the reader, giving both a summary of the plot and an outline of events. In this respect, these early *libretti* preceded programmes. Although modern programmes may not be quite as complete as their predecessors, it is usual now for record companies to provide a full libretto with a translation into several languages, with each set of opera tapes, or discs.

A libretto might be a completely original work, or one adapted from an existing literary work. Sometimes the music has come first, sometimes the words. There have been famous partnerships between librettist and composer throughout the ages, for example, Da Ponte and Mozart, Gilbert and Sullivan, but some composers, like Wagner and Tippett, have preferred to write their own words. Yet again, some libretti, for example, those by Metastasio, have been set many times over by different composers.

PIETRO METASTASIO (1698–1782)

A child prodigy who wrote his first tragedy at the age of 14, this Italian poet went on to become the most frequently set librettist of all time. Apart from his other work, Pietro Metastasio wrote 27 full-scale opera libretti and these would be set many times over by different composers.

Metastasio was perfectly in tune with the requirements of *opera seria*, yet managed to keep on the best of the Baroque traditions, such as placing the utmost significance on the use of words to convey emotions; at the same time, he preserved the objective and dignified requirements of opera seria.

Metastasio made things easier for composers by putting a structure into place, so that, in most cases, a certain number of characters, reflecting a selection of voice types, would play the required solo and subsidiary roles. This type of 'formula' writing allowed composers to demonstrate their versatility within a logical plan.

Metastasio was considered to be the greatest poet in Italy and viewing his achievements through contemporary eyes, it seems apparent that he was not simply an outstanding poet of his times, but also a skilled and effective professional writer.

Set design

The visual spectacle of opera can be as thrilling as the music itself; a fact that has not been lost upon some of history's most significant artists and designers. Opera design has been influenced by many schools of art and has benefited from the input of designers from a variety of artistic backgrounds.

Some of the forms of entertainment preceding opera, such as masques, involved complex machinery and elaborate scenery and these crowd-pleasing effects were attractions in their own right. In opera, design became an intrinsic part of the whole rather than a separate diversion and so the balance changed.

The earliest operas, in keeping with the intention to resurrect the directness of ancient Greek theatrical principles, often had simple settings, but in the seventeenth century rivalry between various courts drove theatre development forwards, towards a scheme we would recognise today; tiers of seats, boxes, and the proscenium arch, separating the audience from the proceedings on-stage. Eye-catching sets complementing the action were an obvious requirement. No expense was spared in these theatres, whether to obtain more and better musicians, more elaborate costumes, or more intricate and fantastic stage machinery. In public theatres, which needed to pay their way, savings had to be made. Last on the list of economies was set design. Cloud machines and 'magical' transformations, which relied heavily upon sophisticated lighting, were essential if the man or woman in the street was to be wooed into these theatres. This public expectation fuelled the development of set design and it became an artform in its own right.

Designers

The first designer to achieve widespread recognition was an Italian called Bernado Buontalenti (1531–1608). Translated into English his last name means 'great talent'; this may have been a nickname, or just a fortunate coincidence. An architect and designer, Buontalenti worked for the Medici family in Florence, creating designs for both buildings and stage spectaculars. His designs for early opera were reputedly as visually splendid and as mechanically unobtrusive as could be hoped for.

Giovanni Burnacini (c. 1605–55), the designer believed to have staged some of Monteverdi's operas, continued the development of stage machinery, passing on the task to his son, Ludovico, 1636–1707. Several other Italian families were also prominent in theatrical design around this time. The Galliaris, the Galli-Bibienas and the Mauros, were among the most significant. These skilled men all helped to push forward the boundaries of what was theatrically possible, imposing excellence upon the finished product. The Quaglio dynasty carried the excellence of Italian design to Germany. From the birth of Giulio Quaglio in 1601, this Italian family's lineage may be traced through six generations and boasts no fewer than 15 designers. From the operas of Gluck, through to those of Mozart, Beethoven and Wagner, this remarkable group continued to leave their mark on opera design.

Throughout the nineteenth century, designers such as the German architect, Karl Schinkel (1781–1841), whose grasp of perspective and fine attention to detail allowed him to handle large, complex projects, and the French painter, Pierre-Luc-Charles Ciceri (1782–1868), who, amongst his other proficiencies, was the first to use a moving panoramic backcloth at the rear of the stage, continued to bring into prominence the exciting visual possibilities of opera.

At the same time, a greater concern for historical accuracy was asserting itself, alongside which was the influence of nationalism. All the diverse schools of art have been reflected by the designers of the time, and in the twentieth century a sense that there were many ways in which a work might be depicted was growing. The Russian designer, Alexandre Benois (1870–1960), thrilled the public with his bold use of colour and spectacular designs. The Swiss designer,

Adolphe Appia (1862–1928) chose a more abstract route to visual interpretation. Using set design and especially lighting in a more imaginative way than ever before, Appia attempted to convey an emotional state, rather than simply a visual reality. This abstraction made his style ideal for the works of Richard Wagner and he was responsible for the Milan production of *Tristan und Isolde* in 1923 and for the Basle productions of *Das Rheingold* and *Die Walküre* in 1924–5.

Another German, Emil Preetorius (1883–1973), sought to interpret the Wagnerian operas using a combination of symbolism and quasi-reality, the same qualities he found in the music.

Richard Wagner's grandson, Wieland Wagner (1917–66), continued the abstract approach when he took over, with his brother Wolfgang, the business and artistic administration of his grandfather's operas at Bayreuth. Wieland based his designs upon lighting, rather than scenery, thus stressing the intensity, internalism and mythical qualities of the operas.

Not that opera design has always to be deeply introspective to be valid. Designers from a variety of different artistic backgrounds have made their own, equally valuable contributions to the way that opera is perceived and enjoyed. Fashion photographer Cecil Beaton, the artist and cartoonist Osbert Lancaster, the famous French artist and cartoonist Romain de Tirtoff Erte, well-known ballet designer Oliver Messel, the film makers Visconti and Zeffirelli, the artist David Hockney, are amongst many who have helped, through their varied, fascinating and sometimes flamboyant interpretations, to bring opera to a wider audience than ever before.

DAVID HOCKNEY

Born in Bradford in 1937, David Hockney brings wit, exuberance and drama to his artwork generally, and made an easy transition to the theatre. His talent in this area was fully revealed when he designed both costumes and sets for Alfred Jarry's *Ubu Roi*, a play shown at London's Royal Court Theatre in 1966.

It was another eight years before Hockney accepted a major commission from the world of opera. This was for the

Glyndebourne production of Stravinsky's *The Rake's Progress* in 1975. The stage director was John Cox, who was also to direct the 1978 Glyndebourne production of Mozart's *The Magic Flute*, which again benefited from David Hockney's outstanding designs. The next important commission came from the Metropolitan Opera House in 1979. This event, an evening devoted to twentieth-century French theatre, was such a huge success that Hockney's renown as one of the greats amongst theatrical designers was assured.

Recordings versus live performance

All the most popular operas will be available on several recordings. Specialist magazines and critiques in newspapers will provide an overview of some of these, and you can also find guidance in a book such as the *Penguin Guide to Opera on Compact Discs*. Alternatively, a record store specialising in classical music should have someone on hand to advise you. Remember that today's technology allows difficult passages to be reworked and added later if necessary, with even an individual note being spliced into existing music. Don't take this expectation of absolute perfection into a live performance, where the overall experience is perhaps more satisfying in some ways than a recorded performance, however flawless.

Acts and scenes

An act is a major subdivision in an opera. It may form a complete dramatic whole with a proper ending, rather like the ending of a chapter in a book. Each act may be divided up into a number of scenes. This format originated in Greek drama where the entrance of the chorus defined sections of the unfolding drama. The earliest operas of the sixteenth century could have as many as five acts.

By the mid seventeenth century, three acts were usual, although the French composers preferred the classical five-act structure, as did, for example, Verdi in his opera *Don Carlos*. *Opera buffo* on the other hand, might have only two acts, and there are some miniature gems with just one act, for example Mascagni's *Cavalleria Rusticana*. Richard Strauss wrote full length operas in a single act.

The number of scenes within an act may vary according to the interpretation of a particular director. Large scene (scenery) changes used to be confined to the intervals between acts, but with the advent of modern technology, relatively smooth transformations can take place more speedily, adding vastly to a director's scope for change of mood, between, or even during a scene.

The pendulum of etiquette has swung back and forth during opera's history. Customs also vary according to country and particular venue. In some places, it is considered correct to wait until an act is completed before applauding, whereas in others, anything goes!

——— Who else is involved? ———

The performance on-stage reveals just the tip of an iceberg. This final realisation of any composition requires the involvement of numbers of unseen hands before it reaches the public domain. The general management team, front-of-house staff, stagehands, sound and lighting engineers, stage management, wardrobe, wigs, armourer – you might be carrying a spear, but it has to be one from the appropriate historical period – and myriad other providers are essential if opera is to survive and thrive. All of this costs a great deal of money and the final ingredient, without which none of this would exist, is of course the enthusiastic support of you and me, the general public.

MAXIMISING YOUR ENJOYMENT

When you visit an opera for the first time, the programme is often a useful source of background information. Brief biographies introduce you to the performers, designer and director, allowing you to identify with the real people who are about to offer their unique interpretation for your approval.

You may have read, or heard about other performances of the same work; perhaps it was a total disaster, and while you are waiting for the curtain to rise, you could try to imagine how that audience felt, and wonder if contemporary tastes have become more tolerant; comparisons always prove good talking points.

If you know something of the plot and a little about the period and culture from which the work comes, and if you are familiar with the composer and perhaps a few of his other works, the jigsaw really begins to take shape. This background reading and research may take up a few minutes of your time, but it will add immensely to your enjoyment.

2

HOW LONG MUST I WAIT?

One of the criticisms most frequently levelled at opera regards the amount of padding that seems to prolong the proceedings for no good reason. Lengthy passages of unintelligible **recitative** breaking up the more appealing music can be tedious, especially if you don't understand the language. Getting hold of a translation beforehand, from either the score, CD package, or explanatory notes inside the programme, all helps, but the fact remains that some operas, just like some novels, take longer to make their point than others. If you find yourself not absorbed in either the style, musical performance, story or spectacle, the fact that the particular opera you have chosen to see is generally highly regarded will be scant consolation. The operas reviewed in this book have been specially chosen as works that will grip you from beginning to end, but there are plenty more. The list below will give you an idea of the length of time you will have to wait to hear the popular tunes. Keep an open mind because you may find that you enjoy the music that surrounds your particular favourites more than you expect.

(N.B. Timings are approximate since productions vary.)

- *Celeste Aida* The fantastic tenor solo from *Aida* by Verdi; only 10 minutes to wait!
- *L'improvviso* Another popular tenor aria from *Andrea Chenier* by Giordano; 20 minutes.
- *Nessun Dorma!* In most productions you could nip in after the interval to hear Verdi's tenor chart topper from *Turandot* at the beginning of Act Three, but you would be missing some tremendous music.

- The mezzo-soprano *Cenerentola*, or Cinderella, has a stupendous solo right at the end of the opera of the same name, but this is Rossini at his best, so there is no need to count the minutes.

- Knowing that you must wait considerably longer than two hours for the exciting *Ride of the Valkyries*, from Wagner's opera, *Die Walküre*, helps to put some perspective into this epic work.

- In contrast, Leoncavallo's operatic gem, *I Pagliacci,* lasts a mere hour and, since the 1890s, has been twinned with an equally entertaining work, *Cavalleria Rusticana* by Mascagni. One of the most famous tenor solos of all, *Vesti la giubba*, (the one with sobs at the end) from *I Pagliacci*, comes after 40 minutes, at the end of Act One.

- Puccini's opera *Tosca* contains some well-known melodies. *Vissi d'arte*, the famous soprano aria is towards the end of Act Two. The opening of Act Three with solo horn and haunting shepherd boy's song, is an inspired foundation for the dramatic development of the final act of this great work. The magnificent tenor aria, *E lucevan le stelle* and the gripping finale is still to come!

—— The long and the short ——

The length of performance varies from opera to opera, but basically they can be divided into the long (Wagner) and the short (almost all the rest)! However, it would be wrong to imagine that every long opera is a forbidden fruit to all save the most learned musicologists. Richard Wagner, for instance, created a sound world of unimaginable splendour and depth, and was certainly an operatic composer of supreme genius. That does not mean that you are on your own if you are not instantly drawn to his particular mode of musical expression, for Wagner was stumped when it came to a way of expressing himself succinctly. Be prepared for a lengthy experience, which may grab you from the first sonorous chord, or may render you unconscious after the first hour or so. The celebrated concert pianist, Hedwig Stein demanded to know why it should be necessary to sit through three hours of music to hear three minutes of tune, but her sentiments were not shared by Verdi, who wrote of Wagner's opera *Tristan und Isolde*, 'This gigantic structure [three-and-a-half hours running time] fills me time and time again with astonishment and awe, and I still cannot quite comprehend that it was written by a human being. I consider the second act . . . to be one of the finest creations that ever issued from a human mind.'

Wagner's musical canvas is vast, his storyline epic and his imagery stunning. Try not to form a snap judgement of this colossus of the operatic world, but give yourself time to become acquainted with his very different scale of things. Try the last act of *Götterdämmerung*, or Act Three of *Siegfried* to begin with, and just take it from there . . . you may still be unmoved, or you may discover a new passion. Above all, don't allow whatever you may read about Wagner the man to colour your impression of Wagner the composer.

The Ring *cycle*

Composer: Richard Wagner.

The first complete *Ring* cycle was performed at the Bayreuth Festspielhaus in August 1876, with Hans Richter conducting. The *Ring* cycle, or tetralogy as Wagner called it, took 26 years to complete and comprises four works:

1 *Das Rheingold*   Running time approximately 2 hours 40 minutes.
2 *Die Walküre*   Running time approximately 3 hours 50 minutes.
3 *Siegfried*   Running time approximately 4 hours.
4 *Götterdämmerung*   Running time approximately 4 hours 15 minutes.

When finances allow, an opera house may stage a performance of the *Ring* cycle. This involves the presentation of each of these four operas on consecutive nights. Together they invoke a mythological world whose story unfolds on a heroic scale. The festival at Bayreuth is still the premier venue for this remarkable masterpiece.

Perhaps no other composer had quite the ego, or available resources of Wagner when it came to creating works that would demand supreme enthusiasm, commitment and the sheer physical endurance of both audience and performers, for certainly operas lasting four hours or more are pretty thin on the ground. All Wagner's operas require large orchestral forces and the singers must therefore possess particularly powerful and resilient voices, in order not only to be heard, but to convey the noble sentiments of the music in a convincing manner.

3

PLACES TO VISIT

Venues for opera have adapted and developed over the centuries, to accommodate the taste and styles of the times. In the early years of opera's development, the general preference seems to have been for young voices, and the scale of works performed was relatively small, calling upon only a few musicians to accompany the singing. Private courts and wealthy patrons provided the venue for these performances, often within the precincts of their own homes.

In the seventeenth century, the appeal and subsequent development of the style called for a venue that was available to the public at large and so the opera house became a reality. These earliest designated buildings appeared first in Italy. The opera house at San Cassiano in Venice, opened its door to the public in 1637 and the success of this, one of the first recorded commercial ventures in the field of opera, proved that demand existed. Since those earliest times, the variety and type of venue has multiplied, embracing custom-built, acoustically flawless constructions and open-air arenas alike. Anywhere with a sense of theatre, or an unlikely setting where a sense of theatre may be invoked, is suitable; from the basement of a one-time textile mill in Saltaire, England, to the vast outdoor arena at Verona, Italy, venues for opera are as diverse as the compositions themselves.

Here is just a small sample of the many venues you can visit. Please remember to check with the venue before you travel that the opera season is underway as varying policies exist.

Covent Garden Opera House, London, UK

The original theatre was opened in 1732 on the site of a convent garden, but this was burnt to the ground in 1808. The second theatre opened in 1809 and was again burnt down in 1856. The present theatre opened in 1858. One of the premier houses in the world, Covent Garden has played host to some of the greatest artistes of all time.

Roman Arena, Verona, Italy

An unique open-air setting, boasting an audience capacity of almost 17,000. The summer seasons at Verona provide a spectacle to exceed all your expectations.

Teatro alla Scala (La Scala), Milan, Italy

Built in 1778, La Scala's fame increased as it premiered works by composers such as Rossini, Donizetti and Meyerbeer. Enjoying a golden age in the late nineteenth and early twentieth century, under the brilliant, if despotic, hand of the conductor Arturo Toscanini, La Scala remains one of the foremost venues for opera. Milan's opera season is during the winter months.

Metropolitan Opera House, New York, USA

The Met' opened originally on Broadway in 1883. After a fire, to which opera houses seem predisposed, the theatre was rebuilt in 1892. The new Met' opened in the Lincoln Centre in 1966. Attracting all the tyros of the operatic world, the Met' has also been instrumental in forwarding the careers of many outstanding American singers including Richard Tucker, Leontyne Price, Margaret Harshaw, etc.

Glyndebourne, Lewes, Sussex, UK

An idyllic setting, where dressing-up and picnics on the lawn have become an intrinsic part of the whole experience. Situated in the grounds of the Christie family's home, this festival of opera first began in 1934. The intimate surroundings of the original theatre lent themselves perfectly to the operas of Mozart, but now the repertoire is much larger. Several extensions and renovations have led, in the

1990s, to the construction of an enlarged, custom-built opera house. The season lasts approximately from mid May to mid August, when Glyndebourne on tour allows more people to enjoy the very high standards promoted by this company.

Salts Mill, Saltaire, Yorkshire, UK

A truly unique experience set in the heart of Yorkshire. Once a thriving mill town conceived and developed as a total living and working environment, by the nineteenth-century textiles magnate, Sir Titus Salt, Saltaire has become home to one of the finest exhibitions of the works of the artist, David Hockney. Stone walls ring now, not with the noise of machinery, but the melodies of opera recordings and the air is full of the scent of fresh flowers, as the gallery provides a complete sensory experience for the visitor. The drama of the surroundings has led to actual productions, with for example graffiti artists drafted in to transform the basement of the mill for a production by Opera North (whose home base is the Grand Theatre, Leeds) of *West Side Story* by Leonard Bernstein.

Salzburg Festival, Aust*ia*

The first Mozart festiv*al* *wa*s held in Salzburg, the composer's birthplace, in 1842, altho*ugh* *th*is quaint and lovely city, on the banks of the river Salzach, *play*ed host to some of the earliest opera productions outside Ita*ly. t*he entire city seems infused with music at any time of year *and* *th*e festival attracts international musicians of the highest cal*ibre*.

Oper*a, Pa*ris, France

R*ecentl*y the **Opera Bastille**, this most important of French operatic *instit*utions has undergone various changes of venue and name. It was *in* 1669 that Robert Cambert and Abbé Perrin received permission *f*rom Louis XIV to produce operas in the Italian style, to be sung in French. A strong emphasis on ballet and the emergence of the Grand Opera in the nineteenth century, helped to create a recognisable national style.

Bayreuth Festival, Germany

Like Salzburg, this town, now predominantly associated with one
composer, has been connected with opera since the earliest days.
Authorities in Bayreuth provided land for the Festspielhaus, where
the operas of Richard Wagner could be performed, and *Das Rheingold*
opened in 1876, launching the first-ever complete *Ring* cycle.

Gran Teatro Liceo, Barcelona, Spain

This theatre opened in 1847, but burnt down in 1861. It was rebuilt,
thanks to a share issue of 1,000 shares, and descendants of those
original shareholders still own the theatre. The present house opened
in 1862 and has nurtured the development of many notable Spanish
singers, including José Carreras, Montserrat Caballé and Victoria de
los Angeles.

Aldeburgh Festival, Suffolk, UK

Founded in 1948 by the composer Benjamin Britten, the tenor Peter
Pears and the writer and librettist Eric Crozier, this festival centred
around the preferences and works of Britten. **Snape Maltings** opened
in 1967, to house larger events.

The Sydney Opera House, Sydney, Australia

Considered an extraordinary and futuristic building at the time of its
construction, this house enjoys perhaps the most spectacular setting
of all, in Sydney harbour. Opened by Elizabeth II in 1973, this costly
edifice contains both a concert hall and an opera theatre.

An introduction to opera:
self-test questions

1 At what point in an opera will you hear overture?
2 Name some responsibilities of the conductor.
3 Name one famous conductor and list a few facts about him.
4 Which female and which male voice has the lowest pitch?
5 What was a castrato? Name one outstanding castrato.
6 By what other name was the soprano Jenny Lind known?
7 What nationality was Feodor Chaliapin?
8 What function is performed by the librettist?
9 Name one famous set designer.
10 Might there be several acts in a scene, or several scenes in an act?
11 From which opera does the aria *Celeste Aida* come?
12 How many operas are there in Richard Wagner's *Ring* cycle?

Part Two

ON WITH THE SHOW
THE HISTORY
OF OPERA

4

THE BIRTH OF OPERA

The power of song can be traced back to antiquity and the process of presenting a musical drama has been a constantly evolving process making it difficult to pinpoint an exact birth date for the style known as opera.

In the sixteenth century it was customary for interested parties from the intelligentsia and aristocracy to get together on a regular basis to discuss, amongst other subjects, how best to advance the arts. One such group met at the home of **Count Giovanni de' Bardi** in Florence and became known as the **Florentine Camerata** (Florentine Society). Members of this group included:

Jacopo Corsi (1561–1601), amateur musician.

Vincenzo Galilei (c. 1520–91), father of the famous astronomer, Galileo Galiliei, and musician (lutenist, composer, teacher, philosopher), largely responsible for debates concerning artistic practices in ancient Greece, following his discussions with the Italian humanist and musician, Girolamo Mei (1519–94).

Piero Strozzi, amateur musician.

Jacopo Peri (1561–1633), composer, singer, harpist.

Giulio Caccini (1551–1610), composer, singer, lutenist, harpist, teacher.

Emilio de Cavalieri (1550–1602), composer, organist, dancer, administrator, diplomat, teacher.

Ottavio Rinuccini (1562–1621), librettist.

Given the mood of the times, the raw ingredients brought by this group to the home of Count Bardi, were exactly those required to provide a cradle for opera.

To bring about a musical entertainment complete in itself and with a sustained narrative, between them they developed the art of *recitativo*, a sung speech-style that allowed the drama to continue between song and musical interludes. This sung speech was relatively free, allowing the meaning of the words to be delivered convincingly, and was accompanied unobtrusively by music that followed, rather than led, the singer.

To fully appreciate the heritage these men were building on, it is necessary to travel back further still.

—— Some early performers ——

Jongleurs or minstrels were professional performers, dating from about the tenth century, who were the travelling players of their day. Moving about to wherever the work might be, they earned a precarious living with their song, dance, tricks and performing animals. By the eleventh century, some of these groups had formed themselves into guilds, enabling skills to be honed and carried forward to the next generation, rather like teachers in a modern conservatoire. These traditions became the breeding ground for secular music in Europe, and the body of work now known as the music of the troubadours, or *trouvères*.

The German *Minnesinger* was a noble poet-musician whose catalogue of work was rather more serious in nature. Concerned largely with love, the music of the Minnesinger might be religious or sensual and flourished between the twelfth and fourteenth century. After the Minnesinger, came the *Meistersinger* (see *Die Meistersinger von Nürnberg* by Richard Wagner), usually German artisans, whose guild of Meistersingers survived until the nineteenth century.

—— Europe in the fifteenth and sixteenth centuries ——

In the late fifteenth and early sixteenth century, the most highly developed European cultures looked back longingly at the artistic world of early Roman and Greek civilisations (see 'Constantinople'). Although it wasn't possible to be certain exactly how the music of these times had sounded, it was possible to read ancient manuscripts, detailing the profound effect the compositions and performances of the best musicians had made upon the listener. The feeling that it was both possible and desirable to recapture these ancient skills swept across Europe.

The Church

The medieval Church was quick to seize upon the notion that the Christian message could best be communicated to the masses by way of an entertainment. These plays, with music, costume and scenery are known to have existed in Europe as early as the tenth century and contain all the bare essentials for opera.

Morality plays (concerned with virtues and vices), mystery plays, (stories from the scriptures), miracle plays, (stories concerning lives of the saints), or *Sacre Rappresentazioni* as the last two were known in Italy, were certainly a forerunner of opera. The Sacre Rappresentazioni would have been held in the precincts of the church, or even outside in the Italian sunshine, allowing for some tainting from secular festivals, which in turn caused this dramatic musical style to develop.

Pageants

Secular entertainments, whether to celebrate quasi-pagan festivals such as safely bringing in the harvest, or to mark a significant occasion such as a royal wedding, contained some elements of opera, though a pageant might last for a few hours, or even a few days. In 1483 possibly the most consequential 'set designer' of all time painted the scenery for the spectacular entertainments performed at the wedding of Gian Galeazzo Sforza to Isabella d'Aragon, for this commission was given to the artist Leonardo da Vinci. Another well-documented pageant also celebrated a royal wedding; that of Ferdinando de Medici to Christine of Lorraine in 1589 in Florence. Buontalenti was the designer on this occasion, and a play, *La Pellagrina* (The Pilgrim) formed part of the entertainments. This play contained six *intermedi*, or dramatic musical interludes. One of these, *Il Combattimento pitici d'Apollo col Serpente*

(Apollo's victory over the Python), was later developed by the poet and librettist Ottavio Rinuccini (a member of the Florentine Camerata) and the composer Jacopo Peri (also a member of the Camerata), into the first opera, *Daphne*; first performance, Florence 1598.

The masque

The *masque* was a type of courtly entertainment that flourished in Europe in the sixteenth and seventeenth centuries, surviving into the eighteenth century. In Elizabethan England in particular, great dramatists such as Ben Jonson in collaboration with the designer Inigo Jones, brought the masque to the height of artistic excellence. Involving speeches, poetry, song, instrumental music, dance, games or revels, interplay with the audience and sometimes spectacular scenery and settings, the courtly masque could be an extremely elaborate and costly affair.

A masque might contain some of the elements found in opera, and the performances might also conform to a general theme, but generally speaking the style lacked the continuity of narrative drive.

Constantinople

The capture of this city by the Turks in 1453 caused the dispersal of many Greek intellectuals. These scholars fled to many countries, taking with them valuable manuscripts that would be instrumental in promoting an interest throughout Europe in the culture of the ancient Greeks.

Council of Trent 1545–63

This council, held spasmodically over a number of years in Trent, Northern Italy, was formed in order to undertake a cleansing and ordering of all matters relating to the Catholic Church. With regard to Church music, it was to be free from any hint of sensual or lascivious material; voices were to be sweet and diction clear. No carelessness would be tolerated, by either instrumentalists, who must not play too loud, or by singers, who must maintain a respectful attitude at all times. The long-term effect of these policies, and particularly those regarding choice of material to be performed, meant that there was no longer a place in the Church, either for entertainments containing some secular material, or for musicians and singers who wished to expand their repertoire beyond this narrow band. By pushing out some of the more adventurous performers and composers in this way, the Church helped to promote the development of secular music in the wider world.

SOUND WORLD SIXTEENTH CENTURY

At the beginning of the sixteenth century written music for *intermedi* and the earliest operas would have been in the form of vocal scores with a figured bass. This last term means a bass line written out for the instruments taking the lowest notes, to include some symbols and figures to suggest possibilities apart from the bass, or vocal line, that might be played by other instruments.

Instrument making was quite a sophisticated art, with families of instruments being created at one time to ensure an evenness of tone throughout the range, from bass to soprano. Recorders, shawms (a double-reeded wind instrument made in seven sizes, from treble to bass) and viols (a family of string instruments, similar to the violin family although having a fretted neck and six strings, to be played without vibrato), are just three families for which this technique would be employed. A consort of viols, for instance, refers to a complete set, ideally matching i.e. made together. Other popular instruments of the time included the organ, the clavichord, harpsichord, the sackbut (an early trombone), the cornett and the transverse flute. A full-bodied tone, even throughout the range, was liked, although the lute, one of the most popular household instruments of the time, was capable of producing sounds of the greatest subtlety and expression.

The birth of opera: self-test questions

1 What was the Florentine Camerata?
2 There were eight main members of the Florentine Camerata. Name them.
3 Name at least two early groups of professional singers.
4 How did the Church affect the development of musical dramas?
5 A masque could form part of a pageant; what was a masque?
6 The fall of Constantinople promoted European interest in ancient Greek culture; why?
7 What was the Council of Trent set up for and how did it aid the development of secular entertainment?
8 Name and describe three instruments common to the sixteenth century.

5

ITALIAN COMPOSERS LEAD THE WAY

Giulio Caccini (1551–1610)

Renowned for his compositions, Giulio Caccini was also one of the most celebrated singers of his day. He served at the Medici court in Florence, at the Tuscan court and also spent several months in Paris. If Galilei gave the ideas of the Florentine Camerata a literary airing in his treatise *Dialogo della musica antica e della moderna* (Dialogue on music ancient and modern), his fellow Camerata member, Caccini, was one of the first musicians to put the theorising into practice. Calling for a 'noble negligence' in the singing of his airs, Caccini introduced a collection of songs in 1601 entitled *Le Nuove Musiche* (The New Music). His idea was to move away from the ornate embellishments that had become so fashionable and, in keeping with the principles of the Camerata, return to a direct and affecting simplicity. This fresh approach was to be called, *Seconda prattica* and with its new, freer style, allowed the voice to be used as a vehicle for dramatic expression.

Jacopo Peri (1561–1633)

Described as 'a most exquisite singer', by his contemporary Marco da Gagliano, court composer to the Medici, Jacopo Peri, like his colleague Caccini, brought both the skills of a composer and the art of the singer to further the cause of the 'new music'. Also a musician at the court of the Medicis, Peri was famed as *Il Zazzerino* (The man with the long hair), on account of his flowing, gold locks. His setting of

Rinuccini's libretto, *Daphne*, in which he collaborated with the nobleman and fellow member of the Camerata Jacopo Corsi, is now generally regarded as the 'first' opera.

Peri took the leading role of Apollo and the first performance was given at the home of Jacopo Corsi in Florence.

As part of the wedding celebrations of Henry IV of France to Maria de Medici in 1600, Peri was asked to write a piece for public performance and this commission resulted in the opera, *Euridice*. Once again, Rinuccini provided the libretto and Peri took the leading role of Orpheus. Interestingly enough, some of the music was rewritten by his colleague, Giulio Caccini, before the first performance. Accompaniment was provided by lutes, other string instruments and by a harpsichord, although these were kept out of sight of the audience, behind the scenery. The music for this opera has survived and any modern revival demonstrates the strength of the work, although it would surely have been doubly effective when one of the leading roles was taken by Jacopo Peri, its composer, about whose performance on this notable occasion, Marco de Gagliano said, 'I shall not go to the trouble of praising it, since everyone praises it to the skies, nor is there any lover of music who does not keep *Orpheus*' songs before him at all times'.

PERI SINGS, THEN THROWS HIMSELF INTO THE SEA ...

It would appear that apart from his undeniable talents as both singer and composer, Jacopo Peri was something of a 'ham'. During the wedding celebrations for Fernando de Medici and Christine of Lorraine in 1589, he appeared in the musical intermedi to a comedy play. During the fifth intermedi, Peri appeared, seated at the stern of a 'ship', in the guise of the poet-singer, Arion. Having sung a piteous lament of his own composing, Peri upped and threw himself, fully clothed, into the 'sea'. A great howl and a splash followed, then, after a suitable pause, the great man returned triumphant, carried aloft by two friendly dolphins.

Claudio Monteverdi (1567–1643)

If Caccini and Peri were delicious appetisers for the New Music, Claudio Monteverdi provided the main course. Born in Cremona, Italy, this composer served the court of Mantua and was later maestro di cappella at St Mark's, Venice. Master of the 'old style' and fully conversant with the 'new', Monteverdi also proved himself a master of public taste, fully able to adapt his skills to provide whatever was required for a particular occasion.

Achieving this without compromising his genius allowed this composer to elevate the New Music to previously unrealised heights.

At the age of 39 and with an established reputation, Monteverdi presented his opera, *L'Orfeo* in honour of Prince Francesco Gonzaga in Mantua, in 1607. Taking Rinuccini's setting of *Euridice* as his inspiration, the poet Alexandro Striggio had expanded the work into a five-act drama and Monteverdi's orchestra too underwent a similar expansion. Some 40 instruments were called upon at various times, including a complete string section, flutes, cornetts, sackbuts, trumpets, a wooden pipe organ, together with several other instruments to provide continuo. Even more interesting was the fact that now Monteverdi stated clearly which instruments were to be used at precise times throughout the work. Monteverdi's reputation as the foremost composer of opera in his day was confirmed the following year, when he was commissioned to write a work to form part of the celebrations for the wedding of the same Francesco Gonzago, to Margherita of Savoy. Marco da Gagliano, whose own work, *La Dafne*, was also presented during the wedding festivities, wrote of Monteverdi's *Arianna*, 'Monteverdi, a most celebrated musician and chief of his Highness's music, wrote the airs so exquisitely that one may truthfully aver that the virtues of ancient music were reborn, for all the audience were visibly moved to tears.' He goes on then to give a perfect definition of opera, saying that *Arianna* contained, 'all the noblest pleasures, such as the invention and treatment of the tale, sense, style, sweetness of rhyme, musical artistry, consorts of voices and of instruments, exquisite beauty of singing, comeliness in the dancing and gestures and ... no small part is played therein by painting ... scenic perspective and the costumes, so that together with the intellect, all the noblest senses are gratified at once.'

In addition to an extensive catalogue of both sacred and secular music, more operas were to come, and with his last, *L'incoronazione di Poppae*, Monteverdi achieved his masterpiece. Though lacking the scenic sophistication and large orchestral forces of *Orfeo*, this opera set new standards for the depiction of human emotions through the medium of music. *L'incoronazione de Poppae* is just as powerful in performance today, and together with the rest of his work, shows Monteverdi to be one of the prime movers in the advancement of opera style.

Venetian opera

A group of players that had already enjoyed some success in Rome was significant in the development of Venetian opera. Benedetto Ferrari (c. 1603–81), a composer and librettist also famed for his mastery of the theorbo, a large member of the lute family, together with the singer and composer, Francesco Manelli (1594–1667), worked together to produce the opera, *Andromeda*, at the Teatro San Cassiano in Venice in 1637.

This production was a landmark in the development of opera since it was the first to be shown on a commercial basis; a daring project, as previously opera had enjoyed the support of some wealthy member of the aristocracy. *Andromeda* was produced on a tight budget though fortunately, Manelli was able to play two of the leading roles and his wife, also a singer, played another. Six singers, three of whom were castrati, and 12 musicians, made up the company, with Ferrari, the librettist, doubling as a musician. In spite of these cost-cutting exercises, no economies were made where spectacular stage effects were concerned, for without these, the paying public might not come.

The success of this venture was a significant step in the continuing progress of opera, for by making the style available to a wider audience, its future was guaranteed. A second public opera house opened in Venice just two years later, and by 1700 at least 15 more opera houses had opened in that city alone.

❢ Would you know what an opera is? It is an odd medley of poetry and music, wherein the poet and musician, equally confined one by the other, take a world of pains to compose a wretched performance. ❢

Charles de Marguetel de Saint-Denis, Seigneur de Saint Evremond (1610–1703)

The Venetian passion for opera was by no means an universal trend, as the previous account by a famous French wit and courtier shows. The French in any case were particularly dismissive of opera in the early days, since their theatres boasted dramatic productions of great sophistication. In these entertainments, however, music was merely an incidental feature. St Evremond goes on to praise some of the individual qualities of opera, but remarks loftily that 'the 'wonderful' is very tedious where the mind has so little to do.' This scathing attack on the style was taken up by other detractors and could be said to have bedevilled opera ever since.

PERFORMANCE ADVICE

Advice given to performers in Renaissance times is just as relevant today!

Gioseffo Zarlino (1517–90) was both a priest and a musician. His famous treatise, *Le institutioni harmoniche*, contained a section offering advice to the singer, of whom there were many, since ten singers could be employed for the same cost as one lutenist.

'the singer must aim diligently to perform what the composer has written,'

'a singer should not force the voice into a raucous, bestial tone,'

'each vowel sound should accord with its true pronunciation,'

And perhaps most importantly …

'singers should refrain from bodily movements and gestures that incite the audience to laughter'.

Italian composers lead the way: self-test questions

1 Giulio Caccini produced a significant song collection. What was this called and how did the songs differ in the main from the fashionable style of the time?
2 As what did this new style become known?

3 Jacopo Peri excelled as both performer and composer. He took
leading roles in two of his own operas. Name the operas and the
roles taken by Peri.

4 How do you view Claudio Monteverdi's importance in the
development of opera?

5 Name the first commercial opera house and the city in which it
existed?

6 What was the first opera to be presented at this opera house?

7 In the main, who financed opera before this time?

6

THE SECOND HALF OF THE SEVENTEENTH CENTURY

SOUND WORLD SEVENTEENTH CENTURY

As difficult as it may be to believe today, in the seventeenth century the violin was a controversial instrument. On the one hand, the French academic Marin Mersenne (1588–1648) praised the instrument as representing the 'ideal' vehicle for producing a sound totally in accord with Baroque taste, yet on the other hand, being associated with all things Italian, the violin met with considerable disfavour in some other French circles. This rivalry between instruments of the French court, such as the viola da gamba, which produced a more mellow sound, and the violin, was to preoccupy scholars for some time until the violin finally emerged the victor. This victory was made more certain by a group known as 'the twenty-four violins of the King', established at the French court in the late sixteenth century. This group consisted of 6 violins, 12 violas and 6 cellos, and performed together with a group of some 12 wind instruments.

As an adjunct to this type of more organised force, many composers were now writing music for specific instruments, and particular musical forms were being established and becoming recognisable in composition.

Britain

At the beginning of the seventeenth century, the masque flourished at the courts of James I (reign: 1603–25) and the early part of the reign of Charles I (reign: 1625–49).

In the mid seventeenth century, Britain suffered a civil war (1642–9), and became a commonwealth (1649–60). Strict prohibitions enforced during this puritanical era forbad stage plays, but did allow performances containing some sung music, for they could be termed concerts. William Prynne, Arch-Puritan, to whom masques and plays were 'the work of the devil', conceded that, 'music of itself is lawful, useful and commendable.' This ensured that the idea of sung dramas was not extinguished completely in the 11 years of the Commonwealth. When Charles II was restored to the throne in 1660, all unreasonable bans on performance were removed, allowing previously suppressed talent to flourish.

Following the restoration, two major works emerged that were sung throughout. The first, John Blow's *Venus and Adonis* (c. 1682), was called by him, 'a masque for the entertainment of the King', yet closely followed the operatic style.

The second, Henry Purcell's *Dido and Aeneas* (1689), is the first surviving English opera, but its composer was to die in his middle thirties, before having a chance to establish an English operatic tradition.

France

Although the influence of Italian culture upon the French could be said to go back further than 1600, the influence of Italian opera can be traced back to the marriage of Maria de Medici to Henry IV of France, which took place in Florence in 1600. On this occasion the performance of Peri's opera, *Euridice*, made such a great impression upon the bridal couple that the librettist, Rinuccini, later received several invitations to attend their court in Paris, and was even appointed a Gentleman of the King's Bedchamber.

Various attempts to establish Italian opera in France were made throughout the first part of the seventeenth century, but the French already possessed a strong theatrical tradition of ballet and drama and were reluctant to embrace the new style.

The first French composer to write a successful opera was Robert Cambert. *Pomone*, staged at the Salle du Jeu de Paume de la Bouteille in 1671, found favour immediately since it managed to combine all the elements so loved by the French public, namely special effects, dance, classical French tragedy, song, and Cambert also contrived a form of recitative that allowed the French language to be expressed with greater eloquence than ever before.

Noting the burgeoning interest in opera, the ever-astute composer, Jean-Baptiste Lully, turned his attention to the newly fashionable style. Developing it with the energy and excellence for which he was already famed, Lully took opera to new heights both musically and visually, achieving standards which were admired throughout Europe.

Germany

Italian composers and singers were welcomed into many European cities in the seventeenth century, and Germany's cities were no exception. In 1627, a translated and adapted version of Peri's opera, *Daphne*, was performed on the occasion of a royal wedding in Torgau, Saxony. Responsibility for the musical adaptation was given to the German composer, Heinrich Schutz, and it is not possible to say how much of his own work might have been interpolated into the original. Schutz, a most important German composer of this time, wrote prodigiously for voice and instrument, but no trace remains of any opera which he might have written.

Italy

Enthusiasm for opera continued unabated throughout the century, with Venetian opera houses remaining pre-eminent. The renown of their spectacular performances and glorious music spread across Europe, fuelling interest in the style. Carlo Pallavicino (1630–88) and Agostino Steffani (1654–1728) were two of many significant Italian composers who had both the knowledge and the skill to nurture the new style in foreign courts and Steffani, in particular, is now regarded as an important forerunner of composers such as Handel.

The popularity of opera was gaining pace all over Italy, with Rome enjoying a particular significance under the patronage of the Barberini family. This wealthy family was eventually banished from Rome in 1644 and fled to Paris. Here, with the support of Mazarin, the Italian-born French Prime Minister, the family was responsible for producing some of the first Italian operas to be seen in France.

Solo singing and the *aria* was coming into its own, for there was less demand, or possibly less money available in the new commercial houses for a large chorus. Another factor in the rise of the aria was the limited musical interest to be enjoyed in recitative. The purpose of recitative was to provide a vehicle for the expressive use of words and in this it was successful, but the audience wanted more. Even the orchestra was now usually required to accompany the singers, rather than to provide interludes of its own, so the aria became the focus of musical interest.

In Naples a further development saw a move towards a more direct musical style that allowed the solo voice increased prominence, and this heralded the emergence, in the eighteenth century, of the singer as a major force in his or her own right.

A ROUGH GUIDE TO THE NAMING OF TIMESCALES

Medieval:	approximately 11th century–14th century
Renaissance:	14th century–16th century
Baroque:	16th century–1750 (approximately)
Classical:	late 18th century–early 19th century
Romantic:	19th century–20th century
Contemporary:	20th century onwards

N.B. All periods overlap, and elements of each era are apparent in subsequent works.

Summary of opera developments in the late seventeenth century

- At this time, Italy was the centre of opera development, with Venice the hub of the action.
- Interest in the style was beginning to spread across Europe.
- Visually spectacular productions were extremely popular.
- Vocal virtuosity was a requirement for solo singers wishing to take part in leading productions.
- Due to economic considerations, large choruses in many public opera houses had almost disappeared.
- In the main, the orchestra had little to do but accompany the singers.
- Recitatives contained little of interest musically; expressive use of language important.
- The aria reigns supreme.

– Late seventeenth-century composers –

Henry Purcell (1659–95)

It would be impossible to overstate Henry Purcell's contribution to seventeenth-century vocal music. The tragedy is that he died so young and produced only one opera. In spite of his short life, Purcell composed a great many works and his particular genius, as far as the singer is concerned, lay in his ability to produce the most beautiful and elegant music which, whilst requiring diligence with regard to study and technique, never placed unreasonable demands upon the voice.

Son of a Gentleman of the Chapel Royal, Purcell began his musical career as a chorister at the chapel, moving on when his voice broke to learn the skills of instrument keeper, maker, tuner and repairer. As a young teenager, he was responsible for tuning the organ at Westminster Abbey, and in 1677 he became Composer for Violins at the Chapel Royal. In 1679, he was appointed organist at Westminster Abbey, receiving a wage of £10 a year, and in 1682 was appointed organist at the Chapel Royal. The following year saw him taking over the duties of Keeper of the Instruments at the Chapel Royal at a salary of £60 a year; swift advancement by any reckoning.

Apart from many religious compositions, Purcell wrote songs for the court and in a six-year period, he produced incidental music for more than 40 plays. Four of these works contained so much music that they are now considered by some to be semi-operas.

King Arthur comes closest of these four to resembling opera, and its author, John Dryden, described it as a 'dramatic opera'. This description might have been valid in the arena of seventeenth-century British theatre, but in fact the main characters spoke, rather than sang their lines.

Although he made a thorough study of the Italian style, Purcell did not set any Italian words to music. His musical settings for the English language, however, utterly repudiate the concept of the Italian language being the only acceptable vehicle for song and, had he lived longer, it seems certain that he would have established an English school of opera in the seventeenth century. Unfortunately, there were no other English composers at the time of his death equal to this task.

His one opera, *Dido and Aeneas* is now recognised as a miniature masterpiece. Lasting no more than an hour, and with vocal music in keeping with the abilities of the young voices for whom it was first written, the melodies are timeless. *Dido's Lament* is one of the greatest and most memorable laments ever to be written. Drawing upon an older heritage, the musical form of this aria marks the inevitability of a descent towards death, with its chromatic downward movement of the bass line accompaniment.

In a newspaper article at the time of his death, Purcell is described as being 'one of the most celebrated masters of the Science of Musicke in the kingdom and scarcely inferior to any in Europe'. He was interred with every honour at Westminster Abbey. *The Oxford Dictionary of Music* describes his untimely death as 'a national calamity', and, for the young singer in particular, this is no less than the truth.

Jean-Baptiste Lully (1632–87)

Giovanni Battista Lully was born in Florence, Italy. He travelled to France at the age of 14 to serve at the court of Mademoiselle de

Montpensier. Quickly finding success with his dancing and musical talents, by the age of 21 he entered the service of Louis XIV, as Composer of the King's Instrumental Music. In 1661, Lully adopted all things French and, climbing swiftly up the royal musicians' career ladder, he became Master of Music for the Royal Family.

To begin with, Lully's major compositions were for the ballet, since he, like many others, had yet to be persuaded that the French language was suited to opera and even more significantly for an ambitious young man, the King preferred ballet. Lully's most significant contact, apart from the King whose protection he enjoyed, was the French dancer, actor and playwright, Molière. The Comédie-Ballet which resulted from the collaboration between the two, was a popular combination of singing, dancing, comedy and spectacular effects. General interest in opera was growing, however, and in 1669 the King granted letters patent to Perrin, the librettist, so that he could set up an Académie. In collaboration with Robert Cambert, Perrin produced *Pomone*, now accepted as the first French opera. Although this work enjoyed considerable success, Perrin was not a businessman and encountered acute financial difficulties which resulted in his eventual imprisonment. Seizing the opportunity, Lully, having already purchased the letters patent from his rival, and receiving what amounted to a monopoly over the presentation of opera in Paris from the King, set about the establishment of a truly French style of opera.

His treatment of recitative allowed the French language to be heard and expressed at its best, and dance, rather than the aria as in Italian opera, featured strongly.

A large chorus, a luxury that had almost disappeared in Italy at this time, added a degree of gravitas to the proceedings, and the orchestra achieved a sophistication previously unknown. Building upon the tradition of the court orchestra, or 'twenty-four violins of the King', Lully added other sections as required by the unfolding drama. Woodwind, brass and percussion all had their place in his elegant compositions, and what had previously been a simple musical introduction to a work became the longer and more complex 'overture'.

Visually, the stage presentations were as sumptuous as ever, and texts could be plucked from a rich source, since these were the times of Molière, Corneille, Quinault and Racine. Lully collaborated mainly with Jean-Phillippe Quinault, an important dramatist of this period.

More than simply a composer of operas, Lully was a shrewd entrepreneur who supervised most aspects of his productions. When *Armide* received an unexpectedly cool reception, he declared that he was quite prepared to stage it for his own benefit with himself as the only audience. The King hearing of this decided that since Lully declared the opera perfect, it must be worth listening to. A special performance was presented to the King, who declared himself charmed, and within days, both the court and the public were enthusing about this exceptional new composition by their favourite composer.

The outcome of the developments brought about by Lully meant that the French were able to enjoy a style of opera uniquely their own, in which traditions were not compromised. Dance, spectacular, elegant performances based upon the finest literary texts, remained, thanks to the supremely confident hand of the Italian Frenchman, Jean-Baptiste Lully.

Alessandro Scarlatti (1660–1725)

Not to be confused with his son, the extraordinary keyboard player and composer of keyboard music, Domenico Scarlatti, Alessandro was an important composer of seventeenth- and early eighteenth-century Italian opera. Born in Rome, his first significant post was that of Musical Director to the self-exiled Queen Christina of Sweden. Later, the Spanish envoy at the court of Naples appointed him to the same post in that city. By this time, Alessandro Scarlatti had already written six operas. He was to remain in Naples for 20 years and claimed to have written some 80 operas during his time there, although this is almost certainly an exaggeration. In fact about 40 works survive from this period.

Returning to Rome where he was employed by Cardinal Ottoboni, Scarlatti was disappointed to find that the Pope disapproved of opera. This caused him to return to Naples in 1708, where he was to compose a further 11 operas, including two of his most successful, *Tigrane* and *Cambise*.

In 1721, his opera *Griselda* moved away from the Venetian style to follow more closely a style that was to become known as opera seria.

The popularity of this more serious approach reached a climax in the early and mid-eighteenth century.

Rather than creating a Neopolitan style of opera, as is sometimes claimed, Alessandro was responsible for establishing opera as a popular artform in Naples. A prolific composer, in addition to his many operas, Alessandro composed no fewer than 500 cantatas, together with many other vocal works and a quantity of instrumental music. His writing for the opera orchestra moved into a new era of expertise, both because of his innate understanding for what combination of instruments might best complement the voice, and for his use of the orchestra to enhance the dramatic mood.

Pier Francesco Tosi (1654–1732)

Although this celebrated castrato singer and teacher lived a generation before reformers such as Gluck, his approach to performance was perfectly in sympathy with the aims of a movement that sought a return to dramatic truth.

His treatise, *Observations on Florid Song* published in 1723, reflected Tosi's contempt for the self-serving, ornate style of singing that had become fashionable and recommended in its place a return to the natural and more affecting style of his youth. These writings provide an insight into the techniques of bel canto singing and warn both the singer against excessive use of ornamentation, and the composer against writing out ornaments for universal use, regardless of the capabilities and inclination of the individual singer.

The advice contained within this treatise is as relevant today as it was almost 270 years ago.

Opera in the late seventeenth century: self-test questions

1 Name one earlier form of entertainment that contained singing.
2 What was significant about Henry Purcell's use of language in his opera *Dido and Aeneas*?

3 Why were the French slow to espouse opera?

4 Jean-Baptiste Lully was a great French composer. Where was he born and how did he make opera more acceptable to the French public?

5 Who was the famous composer of operas, Domenico or Alessandro Scarlatti?

6 What is the name of a famous castrato singing teacher who is said to have promoted the *bel canto* style of singing?

7

EIGHTEENTH-CENTURY OVERVIEW

❝ Today there is but one music in all of Europe ❞
Michel Paul Gui de Chabonon, Paris, 1785

A fascinating century of development in the world arena generally, the eighteenth century saw music moving stylistically from Baroque to Classical and on towards the Romantic era.

The rise of a professional middle class helped to foster an ever increasing demand for new music and this need was exaggerated by lack of a varied library of existing works. Music printing grew apace so that more people became familiar with the most recent developments and the popularity of music burgeoned, creating a milieu where the most gifted composers and performers could only flourish. This was a truly cosmopolitan age, with German kings in Poland, Sweden and England and a German princess, Catherine, Empress of Russia. Apart from these influences, there was a Spanish king in Naples, a French duke in Tuscany, the French writer and philosopher Voltaire serving at the French-speaking court of Frederick the Great of Prussia, and the Italian poet Metastasio employed by the German Imperial court in Vienna. These few examples of cross-cultural impulses form just the tip of the iceberg, for the movement of creative individuals between the different courts and countries of Europe was widespread.

Public interest came to reflect a genuine concern for the rights of the individual and the popularity of Freemasonry, with its thesis of a universal human brotherhood, also spread across Europe. All of these factors contributed towards influencing the direction taken by the music of the day.

SOUND WORLD EIGHTEENTH CENTURY

In this century of intense activity in the field of music composition it is almost impossible to narrow down and codify a typical eighteenth-century sound. Many new styles emerged during the first part of the century and of these, some supplanted whilst others co-existed with the older forms.

Following the principles of Enlightenment, by which the supernatural, along with privilege and other such notions, were eschewed in favour of down-to-earth concepts and freedom for the individual, the ideal sound of the 'new' style of music was one that could be easily understood and enjoyed by all. Excessive ornamentation was, initially, shunned in favour of a clear and direct musical message. The harpsichord held its place for a great part of the century as the instrument most commonly used to provide continuo. An orchestra might be directed by either the leader of the first violins, or by the musician seated at the harpsichord. The orchestra had become quite a sophisticated body, and the violin family was beginning now to supplant the viol, whilst other instruments were constructed with greater care and expertise than ever before. Although some successful combinations of instruments had been established, clear distinctions were not always drawn between what types of passage might be best suited to any particular instrument.

Performers, too, achieved a higher level of technical skill as the demand for musical performances grew, creating an atmosphere of competition between both established and aspiring professionals. In some cases this created a negative impact, when, for instance, popular singers might compete vocally against each other at the expense of the music.

By the middle of the century, many of the 'old' style affectations had crept back, prompting Gluck, in a preface to his opera *Alceste* in 1767, to express his wish to 'confine music to its proper function of serving the poetry for the expression and the situations of the plot'. In order to appreciate the exciting developments in opera at this time, it is helpful to take a brief look at the life and work of some of the most significant composers, for knowing that great minds such as Vivaldi, Rameau, Handel, Hasse, Pergolesi, Gluck and Mozart were involved in the evolution of opera in the eighteenth century, makes the study of this period both interesting and valuable.

Antonio Vivaldi (1678–1741)

Immortalised by his famous *Four Seasons* concerto, Vivaldi wrote more than 40 operas, of which around 20 survive to the present day, including several with libretti by Metastasio, such as *L'Olimpiade*.

Although the concertos are rightly regarded as Vivaldi's most important contribution to music, his operas were extremely popular during his lifetime. They were staged in Venice, the city of his birth, more than those of any other composer and are enjoying something of a revival in the present day.

Trained as a priest, Vivaldi was excused his duties because of illness, allowing him to devote his life to music. For some time he was employed at the Pio Ospedale della Pieta in Vienna. This was an orphanage for girls, where, as was the custom in many such establishments, a thorough musical training was given as part of the general education. Concerts by institutions such as this attracted large audiences, for the standards of performance were known to be extremely high. This provided Vivaldi with a perfect showcase for his work and undoubtedly fuelled his popularity. Today it is hard to imagine the scale of work accomplished by composers like Vivaldi, but then the thirst for new music was almost unquenchable.

Vivaldi received commissions for no fewer than 49 operas and he wrote more than 500 concertos, together with numerous other vocal and orchestral works. He was said to pride himself on the fact that he could compose and write out the orchestral score of a concerto faster than a copyist could write our the individual parts. More than simply a great composer and musical director of the Pio Ospedale della Pieta, Vivaldi was also a theatre manager, impresario, violin virtuoso and teacher, who, whilst making his own unique contributions to the development of opera, also upheld the traditions of Alessandro Scarlatti, which led to the establishment of opera seria.

Opera seria

As the name suggests, *opera seria* (lit. serious opera) cut out the comedy of the Venetian style and devoted itself exclusively to high-minded topics. Meaningful delivery of significant verse and grand productions, with more attention given to the singer, were aspects of this style. Lighter works still existed, but branched off, appearing as *intermezzi* and *opera buffa*. Indeed, Naples was to become the main centre for comic opera in the eighteenth century.

Opera seria lent itself to sumptuous court presentations, where the grand costumes of the courtiers and palatial surroundings were almost at one with the production, for at this time the auditorium would be as brightly lit as the stage. Court operas were often presented to mark some special occasion, and a leading role in opera seria style would be the ideal vehicle with which to pay homage to some noble person. Johann Adolf Hasse (1699–1783), a German-born composer and student of Alessandro Scarlatti, was one of the most important composers of opera seria, although his earlier works, through which he had become immensely popular, contained many comedies.

One of the last 'court composers', Hasse had no need to consider commercial realities. This freedom allowed him, through operas such as *Cleofide*, to raise opera seria to a higher level. The double meanings of eighteenth-century conventions are now the only obstacle to modern revivals, which would inevitably provoke more interest in Hasse's work.

Pietro Metastasio (1698–1782), an Italian poet, is probably the most significant and prolific author whose words were set by composers of opera seria. In 1730, his libretto for *Artaserse* was set by Hasse, an association that was to establish the style beyond question (see p. 17).

Chiefly associated with the court, opera seria was performed in public theatres, but gradually gave way to the increasingly popular opera buffa and *Singspiel*. One of the finest examples of an opera in opera seria style, is Mozart's *La Clemenza di Tito*, 1791.

Jean-Philippe Rameau (1683–1764)

Although tutored by his father in the first instance, Rameau, the most notable French composer of his time, also studied briefly in Italy. His musical treatise, *Traite de l'harmonie* (Paris, 1722) established him as the foremost musical theorist of his day, and he was also a famous organist, sought-after teacher and composer of suites for the harpsichord.

Rameau was 50 before he produced an opera, *Hippolyte and Aricie* (Paris, 1733), and most of the compositions upon which his fame rests were written between the ages of 50 and 56.

French opera had fallen somewhat into the doldrums after Lully, but Rameau revived the style and carried it forwards, using a heightened sense of drama, allowing human emotions to play a role, rather than those of mythological figures. The public warmed to this fresh and more relevant approach, although the music critics and academics of the day were not so enthusiastic, regarding him as far too innovative.

Using the chorus as part of the action was also a new idea and Rameau's collaboration with librettists such as the French poet and playwright, Abbé Simon-Joseph Pellegrin, allowed him to inject a greater emotional content into his works. Interestingly enough, *Castor et Pollux* (1737), now considered to be one of Rameau's greatest works, was the least successful during his lifetime. In 1731, Rameau had been fortunate in attracting the patronage of Alexandre-Jean-Joseph Le Riche de la Pouplinière, the foremost patron of music in France, and he was also to receive a pension from Louis XV. Rameau's long and successful career in which he produced 24 operas and ballets, earned him a well-deserved place as one of the most important composers in the history of French music.

LA POUPLINIÈRE (1693–1762)

A fantastically wealthy individual who further enriched his coffers with shrewd investments and by the office of tax collector, La Pouplinière delighted in furthering the careers of all manner of artistic individuals. With several grand residencies in which to entertain and hold court, he gathered about him many of the renowned figures of the day. Luminaries such as Rousseau, Voltaire, Casanova, together with painters and musicians, all mingled at his salon. Holding regular concerts and with his own orchestra to accompany visiting artists, meant that this great patron of the arts required the services of a musical director. From 1731 to 1753 Rameau held this post. By providing the necessary funds, La Pouplinière was able to transform Rameau's ambition to be a successful opera composer into reality.

George Frederic Handel (1685–1759)

Famed for his oratorios, Handel was also a prolific and successful opera composer. His earliest experience of opera was in Hamburg, as a violinist and later harpsichordist under the great composer/director, Reinhard Keiser.

It was essential at this time for ambitious composers to make their mark in the field of opera composition, and by 1706 Handel had written four operas. His travels then began in earnest and after a brief pause in Florence, he reached Rome at the end of the year.

Opera was frowned upon in Rome and for some time, Handel confined himself to writing religious works. His stay in Rome enriched his writing with subtle influences, and also allowed him to make valuable contacts, both with composers such as Alessandro Scarlatti and also with some of the more notable artistes of the day. More travels and more operas followed. A visit to Naples and later Venice, where the jewel of his Italian period, *Agrippina* was produced, led finally to the procurement of a permanent position as musical director for the Elector of Hanover.

A year's leave of absence was granted almost immediately by the Elector, allowing Handel to visit London, where a selection of his compositions was being performed at the Haymarket to great acclaim.

Finding opera seria all the rage in London, Handel set about composing an opera in this style and *Rinaldo* was produced in just 14 days. Shamelessly borrowing suitable portions from his earlier works, Handel nevertheless scored a great hit with the public, although the work was less well received by the music critics of the day. One such critic, Joseph Addison, who co-founded the *Spectator* in 1711 with Richard Steele, might have been suffering from a bad dose of 'sour grapes' since he had tried and failed to produce a workable English libretto.

Addison derided Handel's use of the famous castrato, Nicolo Grimaldi Nicolini (1673–1732), in a particular scene which the critic thought 'childish and absurd'. Apparently, Nicolini was seen, 'exposed to a Tempest in Robes and Ermine, and sailing in an open Boat upon a Sea of Paste-Board'. Handel brushed off the attack and the opera went on to be a huge success, both in London and in Dublin.

In 1711 Handel was recalled to Hanover, but the following year managed to secure a second leave of absence in order to continue his career in England. A number of successful operas followed and in 1713, he was awarded a pension for life by Queen Anne. Following Anne's death in 1714, Handel found himself in disgrace, for his neglected employer, the Elector of Hanover had now become King George I of England. Fortunately for Handel, his talent was such that he was truly indispensable and before long the King had forgiven him, enabling the composer to immerse himself in the development of musical culture in the country he had chosen to call home. The stimulation of the need to produce quantities of operas in an extremely competitive environment, meant that Handel's genius was stretched and exploited to its furthest limit, resulting in a wealth of valuable compositions. Unfortunately, the stylised form of opera seria, combined with the vocal complexity of some of the pieces and the difficulties encountered when attempting to reassign the castrato roles, prevents these works from enjoying wider popularity today.

A uniquely cosmopolitan composer, with his German birthplace, Italian training and English place of work, Handel is now recognised as one of the greatest composers of all time. As far as opera is concerned, he succeeded where others had failed in bringing together the needs of the singers to display their technique to best advantage, whilst sacrificing nothing of the dramatic impetus of a production.

A shrewd businessman and composer of more than 40 operas, Handel turned his back on the style that had brought him so much acclaim, following the premiere of his oratorio *The Messiah* in Dublin in 1742. In this, as with his other vocal works, Handel's use of the chorus surpassed anything previously known and this special gift was noted by the composer Joseph Haydn, who, after hearing the *Hallelujah Chorus* in Westminster Abbey declared, 'He is the master of us all.'

Carlo Brosci (Farinelli) (1705–82)

There were many celebrated castrati, but perhaps the most famous of all was Carlo Broschi, known as Farinelli. This Italian male soprano made his debut in Naples at the age of 15. At 17 he famously entered into a nightly contest during the course of an opera, with a renowned trumpeter in Rome. At first the duel was a light-hearted affair between the two musicians, testing their breath control and technical ingenuity, but the audience were quick to catch on and soon began to cheer on their particular favourite.

Farinelli was to emerge the undisputed champion and news of his amazing abilities spread swiftly. Invitations to sing flooded in and his career was made. Italy remained awestruck by his technical expertise, but Emperor Charles VI of Austria, from whom Farinelli had received many honours for his performances, expressed an opinion that all the musical embellishments and sensational technical displays were actually masking Farinelli's artistry, as well as the composers' musical message. A simpler approach, he opined, would allow Farinelli to reveal the true beauty of his voice, as well as to touch the heart of his audience, rather than simply to amaze them. Farinelli heeded the advice and enjoyed even more success as a result of the contrasts he was able to bring into play now that he was free from the necessity to concentrate solely on vocal display.

He visited England in 1734 and the great musicologist, Dr Charles Burney, described the audience reaction as 'ecstasy,! rapture! enchantment!' The very first note Farinelli sang was executed with such prolonged excellence with regard to dynamic variation, that it was applauded for a 'full five minutes'. Even the orchestra chosen to accompany the virtuoso declared themselves 'disabled', both by astonishment and by awe at his superior accomplishments. Burney concludes that Farinelli possessed such powers as must subdue every hearer, 'the learned and the ignorant, the friend and the foe'. A visit to Spain in 1737 caused such a sensation that King Philip determined to keep Farinelli at his court. A huge sum for the times, amounting to more than £2,000 sterling, ensured the singer's compliance. When Philip was succeeded by Charles III, Farinelli's services were no longer required, but he left Spain with a generous pension, together with much wealth amassed during his service there. He settled in Bologna in 1761, where, having built a substantial mansion, he lived out the rest of his life in great comfort, secure in the affections of an adoring public.

Johann Adolf Hasse (1699–1783)

Like Handel, Hasse was employed for a time in Hamburg by Reinhard Keiser. In Hasse's case, it was his skill as a tenor that brought him to the attention of the great man. A move to Naples allowed Hasse to study with Alessandro Scarlatti, and the operas written during this period brought him great success. In 1730 his opera, *Artaserse* was staged in Venice; in the cast was the famed castrato Farinelli and the equally celebrated soprano Francesca Cuzzoni. The setting of Metastasio's libretto was a bold ploy since the popular Italian composer Leonardo Vinci had set the same libretto and his opera had been presented only one month before Hasse's. Both operas enjoyed great success and would prove crucial to the establishment of Metastasian opera seria in the eighteenth century. Unfortunately, Vinci died shortly after his version was staged, but Hasse was able to capitalise on his success. His next opera, *Dalisa*, was swiftly produced with the Italian singer Faustina Bordoni in the leading role, a further confirmation of Hasse's illustrious reputation, for Bordoni was already established and had enjoyed great success in London, where she had created several roles for Handel. One month after the triumphant premiere in Venice of *Dalisa*, Hasse and Bordoni were married. The couple's fame spread across Europe and hearing of a vacancy at the Dresden court of the Elector of Saxony, Hasse made haste to present his opera *Cleofide* to the court. The combination of Bordoni and Hasse again proved irresistible and Hasse secured the position of court composer.

A court opera was established and, until the siege of Dresden, almost 30 years later, Hasse served the court of Saxony, making him one of the last 'court composers'. After the siege, during which many of Hasse's manuscripts were destroyed, the Elector was forced to disband the opera company, and in 1763 Hasse and his wife moved to Vienna. Here Hasse discovered Metastasio engaged in a dispute with composers such as Gluck, who sought to challenge accepted operatic traditions. Naturally, Hasse backed Metastasio, a move which found favour with the conservative court, once again enabling Hasse to enjoy a secure life of patronage. In 1773 he moved to Venice where he played an active role in the musical life of that city until his death in 1783.

The composer of more than 50 operas, many of which were settings of libretti by Metastasio, Hasse's work was crucial to the development of opera seria. The influence of his work was not confined to Italy and Germany, but spread across Europe; to Paris, for example, which he visited in 1750, and to Poland, where the Electors of Saxony had long-standing historical connections.

> Other composers involved in the establishment of Metastasian opera seria included the Italian Antonio Caldara 1670–1736 and the German Johann Joseph Fux 1660–1741.

Thomas Augustine Arne (1710–78)

Born in London, Thomas Arne developed musical skills in spite of the disapproval of his family. At this time, England was largely an importer of musical expertise and in comfortably-off families, music was generally considered to be an accomplishment, rather than a potential career path.

Handel was certainly active in England at this time, but he was not native born and since the death of Henry Purcell in 1695, there had been no new torch bearers to carry forward the development of English opera. Another factor hindering progress was that the language of the country was not considered appropriate for opera. One form did prosper; the English ballad opera. In the main, this style of entertainment contained popular songs of the time, satirical comment to well-known tunes and parodies of foreign operatic airs.

Arne's first major success was a masque entitled *Dido and Aeneas* (1734). Subsequent to this, he was engaged by the Theatre Royal, Drury Lane, London, where he was to remain for more than 15 years. During this time he composed an enormous number of operas and masques, of which *Comus*, staged in 1738 and featuring Arne's wife Cecilia Young, and his masque *Alfred*, staged in 1740 and containing the imperishable anthem, 'Rule, Britannia', are the most notable.

Artaxerxes, staged in London in 1762, and using a libretto by Metastasio, was to become the only English opera seria to achieve lasting fame.

Arne composed more than 80 works for the stage and contributed music to many others. Some of the songs that have lived on to delight a modern audience, such as 'Where the bee sucks' and 'When daisies pied', originate from his incidental music for the theatre.

Two oratorios, *The Death of Abel* and *Judith* (1761), as well as numerous sacred and secular works, both vocal and instrumental, together with an annual song collection which Arne produced for 20 years, mark him out as one of the most important and prolific English composers of the eighteenth century.

English ballad opera

This style became extremely popular in England following the huge success in 1728, of *The Beggar's Opera*, written by John Gay. The ballad opera was basically a send-up of Italian opera, using popular tunes of the day and parodies of well-known Italian arias to score political points. It was also a useful vehicle for deriding opera, a 'foreign' import that was possibly gaining too much ground for comfort.

The Beggar's Opera

Staged at Lincoln's Inn Fields, London, this was the first really popular example of English ballad opera. Satirising the politics of the day, including the Prime Minister, Sir Robert Walpole, together with Italian opera, this work can be compared in some respects to the much later works of Gilbert and Sullivan. Like the Savoy operas, *The Beggar's Opera* continues to entertain in spite of the fact that its topical commentary has long since ceased to have any real relevance for the audience.

A sequel to the work proved so contentious that all performances were banned by the Lord Chancellor. The words were published, however, and brought John Gay both notoriety and financial success. This piece was staged eventually, almost half a century after it had first been banned, when presumably those victims of its humour were no longer in a position to protest.

—— **The birth of opera buffa** ——

Giovanni Batista Pergolesi (1710–36)

A tragic death from tuberculosis at the age of 26 prevented Pergolesi from enjoying the success of his compositions. In particular, his religious work *Stabat Mater*, completed just days before his death, and the intermezzo, *La Serva Padrona*, written to provide a little light relief between the three acts of his serious opera, *Il prigionier superbo*, have enjoyed popularity to the present day.

The birth of comic opera, or opera buffa, came about through intermezzi such as *La Serva Padrona*, for the customary two lengthy intervals during the three acts of a serious opera lent themselves to the presentation of some lighter form of entertainment. It soon became apparent to composers that it was a more straightforward proposition to present a complete comic work in two acts, rather than to devise two separate and unconnected works for each interval and so the two-act opera buffa was born.

Because secondary works such as *La Serva Padrona* often enjoyed more success than the more serious works into which they were inserted, the comic opera found a ready-made audience eager to espouse this more complete style of intermezzi as an independent form.

Stabat Mater, meaning literally 'His mother stood', was a thirteenth-century poem, taken into the Roman liturgy in the late fifteenth century and later removed by the Council of Trent in 1543–63. Revived in 1727 for the feast of the seven Dolours, (15 September), it was also used as a setting on the Friday after Passion Sunday. There are many settings by Pergolesi, Haydn, Rossini, Dvorak, Verdi and Poulenc.

Amongst the many significant composers of Italian opera in this era, there were three more in particular who helped to spread the popularity of this style across Europe: Niccolo Piccini, Giovanni Paisiello and Domenico Cimarosa.

Niccolo Piccini (1728–1800)

Having studied in Naples with Leonardo Leo, another prolific opera composer, and the influential teacher and composer of sacred works, Francesco Durante, Piccini's first opera, *Le donne dispettose*, staged in Naples in 1754 was an immediate success. During his lifetime, more than 100 operas built on this triumph, including *La buona figliuola*, which is occasionally revived in Italy to this day. *L'Olimpiade*, staged in Rome in 1761, was one of Piccini's most significant examples of opera seria, but it is for opera buffa that he is usually remembered. Invited to Paris in 1776, where it was hoped he would mount a challenge to Gluck's operatic reforms, Piccini never quite managed to achieve the same level of success that he had enjoyed in his native land and in 1789 with the outbreak of the French Revolution, he returned to Naples. The Piccini influence however was far from extinguished in France, since his son, Ludovico, staged works in Paris and his grandson, Louis Alexandre, completed more than 200 compositions for the stage, including 25 comic operas for the French theatre.

Giovanni Paisiello (1740–1816)

Also trained in Naples, Paisiello achieved great success with opera buffa such as *L'idolo Cinese*, staged in Naples in 1767. Paisiello wrote more than 80 operas during his lifetime, including examples of opera seria such as, *Lucio Papirio dittatore*, also staged in Naples in 1767.

In 1776, he was invited to the court of Catherine the Great in St Petersburg, for the express purpose of establishing an Italian opera tradition in Russia. He composed more popular works during his stay, including *Il barbieri di Siviglia*, staged in St Petersburg in 1782. Popular support for this opera was so strong that the composer Rossini was forced initially to choose a different title for his own setting of the work, staged in Rome in 1816: *Almaviva ossia L'inutile precauzione*. Paisiello left Russia in 1784 and after pausing briefly in Vienna, where he composed *Il re Teodoro in Venezia*, he returned to Naples to take up the post of maestro di cappella in the court of Ferdinand IV. Paisiello, together with Cimarosa and Piccini, took opera buffa to its highest point before the genius of Rossini and Mozart took the style into orbit.

Domenico Cimarosa (1749–1801)

One of the most prolific and successful eighteenth century Italian opera composers, Cimarosa excelled in producing popular works in the opera buffa style. Having established a successful career in his own country, he followed the great tradition of his fellow Neapolitans, Nicolo Piccini and Giovanni Paisiello, in furthering the cause of Italian opera in Europe. In 1787 he travelled to St Petersburg where he took over the position of maestro di cappella to Catherine the Great, from another distinguished Italian composer, Giuseppe Sarti. Writing two more operas during this period, *La vergine del sole* and *Cleopatra*, his works were now famous across Europe and in 1791 he travelled to Vienna to take over from Antonio Salieri as Kapellmeister to the court. The following year his opera *Il matrimonio segreto* was so well received there that the cast were famously given a free royal supper in order that they would have the strength to repeat the performance as soon as possible. Cimarosa would relinquish his post to Salieri, returning to Naples to take up the position of maestro di capella to the King.

Welcoming Napoleonic troops into Naples in 1799, however, brought him imprisonment as soon as the Bourbon royal family returned. When eventually he was released, Cimarosa intended to return to St Petersburg, but died in Venice before reaching his destination. Although receiving scant attention today, Cimarosa's renown, as a composer in the opera buffa style in particular, made him as popular as Mozart with some eighteenth century opera lovers.

—— The cult of the singer ——

It is difficult now to imagine how different from today's disciplined excursion a night at the opera in the eighteenth century could be. In Naples for instance, an audience went to see, rather than to hear an opera; more than this, the audience went to see, and be seen. The noise from the public areas as they socialised freely, played cards, ate, drank and even purchased fruit and drinks throughout the performance, scarcely compares with current notions of dutiful attention and respectful silence. Read about eighteenth century audience antics on page 75.

Some parts of the opera were well received, such as dances, spectacle and singers of renown. Lesser players, linking passages, or padding of any description was simply ignored.

All of this helped to foster a breed of 'celebrity' singers whom theatre managers and composers alike could rely upon to seize the attention of an audience. In turn, this led to certain singers misusing the power they wielded. Taking outrageous liberties with the flow of the music or pace of the drama, these artistes would stop at nothing, even demanding that a librettist or composer change, or even insert inappropriate material, if it was likely to further one singer's cause against another's.

These unreasonable demands could only harm opera's cause in the long term, and although there were several issues prompting reform, this abuse of the music by some of the most popular artistes was undoubtedly one of the major factors.

REFORM

Reform demanded that the drama of a piece should be carried forward more realistically (i.e. unhindered by any superfluous vocal, or instrumental activity). The orchestra should play a more important role, both in its own right and as the organ of accompaniment.

After years of neglect, the chorus was once again required to play an intrinsic role in the drama. The prominence of solo singers was henceforth to be balanced with the requirements of the drama.

Some important composers who followed this line include:

- Niccolo Jommelli; Italian, 1714–74
- Tomaso Traetta; Italian, 1727–79
- Christoph Willibald Gluck; German, 1714–87.

Christoph Willibald Gluck (1714–87)

This German composer of Czechoslovakian descent, was forced by parental disapproval to run away from home before he could begin his musical career. Studying firstly in Prague, he then travelled to Northern Italy, where more than ten of his Italian operas would be staged.

In 1745 and now a successful composer in his thirties, Gluck travelled to London, where he met Handel. The following year he recommenced his travels, soaking up musical ideas as he journeyed about Europe, until finally he settled in Vienna in about 1747. Gluck's exposure to musical concepts throughout Europe allowed him to refine and draw upon the best elements of both French and Italian opera. He wrote more than 40 operas of which a few of the most significant will be mentioned, and enjoyed a long and largely successful life that fell into four main phases.

The early years of study
Gluck studied with composers such as Sammartini in Milan c. 1700–75, composing and travelling incessantly before settling in Vienna.

The Vienna period
Gluck's travels continued during this time and in 1748 he left Vienna for two years, visiting Germany, Denmark and Bohemia. More travels, this time to Prague and Naples, culminated with the triumph of his opera *La Clemenza di Tito*, which was a setting of a libretto by Metastasio, staged in Naples in 1752. On his return to Vienna, Gluck accepted the post of Kapellmeister to the Prince of Saxe-Hildburghausen, consolidating his position as one of the foremost composers in Europe.

An invitation to adapt some French operas for presentation at the light-opera house saw Gluck not only responding, but composing some of his own. These were a great success and led to many more commissions, both for public theatres and for the court. An undoubted success in commercial terms, Gluck's significance in the development of opera can begin to be measured by the most important work of this first Viennese period, *Orfeo ed Euridice*. The first of his so-called 'reform' operas, *Orfeo ed Euridice* was staged first in Vienna in 1762, then later revised before being presented in Paris in 1774. The libretto was written by the Italian, Ranieri di Calzabigi (1714–95) and together, Gluck and his librettist sought to rediscover the dramatic truth espoused by the Florentine Camerata more than 150 years before. Their schemes left nothing to chance and the role of *Orpheus* was played by the renowned castrato Gaetano Guadagni, who had studied acting in London with David Garrick.

The opera that enjoyed the most success in Gluck's lifetime was *La recontre imprévue*, written by him in 1764, but this work is less important than others in respect to Gluck's role in the development of opera. In 1767 *Alceste*, another collaboration with Calzabigi, was staged in Vienna and a revised version was presented in Paris in 1776. In the preface, ostensibly written by Gluck, but possibly written by Calzibigi and certainly representing the ideals of both men, a 'beautiful simplicity' was again the aim of this work. Not an immediate success, this further example of Gluck's 'reform' style went on to be highly regarded, and its significance is further increased by the assertions in the preface.

The Paris period

The French public wanted opera in their own language, hence the revision of *Alceste*, and in 1774, this work together with *Iphigenie en Aulide* created a sensation in Paris.

The reason for this lay back in 1752 when the so-called War of the Buffons erupted in response to the unexpected success of an Italian opera company specialising in comic operas. A war of words was waged between self-styled intellectuals, some of whom favoured the Italian style and some who preferred traditional French opera. Jean-Jacques Rousseau went as far as to declare that the French language was unsuited to opera and so the works of Lully and Rameau lost favour, leaving a gap just waiting to be filled by Gluck. The battle was not easily won, and in 1776 the anti-Gluck faction invited an Italian composer, Niccolo Piccinni (1728–1800) to Paris to challenge Gluck's reforms. A vigorous pamphlet and newspaper war was waged between supporters of both actions, until finally the two composers were invited by an enterprising theatre manager to set the same libretto, *Iphigenie en Tauride*. Piccinni's version enjoyed success at the time, but history has proved Gluck's version, produced in Paris in 1779 to be the true masterpiece.

Perhaps weary of all the conflict and certainly unwell, Gluck had already returned to Vienna by the time Piccinni's interpretation of the opera was staged.

The last years in Vienna
Between the ages of 65 and his death at 73, Gluck spent his time in Vienna in ill-health and semi-retirement.

Perhaps even more frustrating for the inveterate traveller was the fact that his travelling days were finally over.

In spite of all his travels and the various influences that contributed towards the development of his musical style, Gluck was essentially a German composer. The passion with which he imbued his music, whilst never losing sight of the impact of unadorned dramatic truth lived on, inspiring composers like Mozart, Weber, Wagner and Richard Strauss.

—— Audiences and the *claque* ——

Today audiences are relatively well behaved, but the tradition of sitting attentively and applauding only at the end of an act is a comparatively recent discipline.

In the eighteenth century, the opera house provided a social assembly point where secrets might be learned, gossip exchanged and business conducted. To the 'high society' of the day, the 'box' was an essential accoutrement. It wasn't considered necessary to pay attention to every on-stage activity, since those off-stage might prove more advantageous. This might appear rather depressing for the performers, but the very fact that opera attracted its audience, for whatever reason, on a nightly basis, led to a well-informed public, who knew when something, or someone was worth listening to, and perhaps almost more crucially for the future of opera, it led to full houses.

The boxes at the opera house in Milan in 1770 are described as having a room leading from each, where refreshments and cards were available. Another area in the building included gambling tables and there were wide galleries where the audience could stroll about, even during the performance if they so wished, changing places freely upon their return.

Things were no better in England, where young men cruised the aisles, talent-spotting, rather as they might in any club these days. To maximise takings, the audience was crammed into every available space, with standing room even allowed on-stage; a custom which seems to have survived to the end of the eighteenth century. One thing is certain, both the performers and the opera had to be outstanding in order to capture the attention of the audience!

By the beginning of the nineteenth century a phenomenon dating from Roman times, known as the *claque* (Fr. smack; clap), had become firmly established in the opera houses of Europe. The claque comprised a group hired by a performer, composer or impresario to influence the response of an audience, by showing either noisy approval or disapproval, as required by their employer. In Paris, potential claque members could even be hired from an agency.

The power of the claque could not be underestimated, as the great Caruso discovered in the twentieth century. He fell foul of this fickle group in his home town of Naples, whilst at the height of his popularity. Making the fatal mistake of not ingratiating himself with the leaders of the local claque, Caruso was greeted with stony silence, then, incredibly, hissed during *Una furtiva lagrima*, one of his most celebrated arias.

Occasionally the claque might consist of unpaid opera groupies, who, priding themselves on their knowledge, would most usually occupy the standing places and pass noisy judgement upon the performers. The outcome for the employer of a claque could not always be assured, as an unfortunate tenor found out at the opera house in Parma when, falling so far short of expectations, he was heartily booed and his money returned. Paid, or unpaid, possessed of artistic integrity, or driven by sheer greed, one thing is certain; the claque has been a powerful and influential force, that even the most famous ignored at their peril.

EIGHTEENTH CENTURY AUDIENCE ANTICS

The many theatres in Venice were noted both for the quality and spectacle of their productions, but not alas for the good behaviour of the local audience. Visitors foolish enough to choose a *parterre* seat situated immediately below the boxes were likely to find themselves spat upon, for this provided a popular diversion during the more tedious moments of an opera.

Eighteenth-century overview:
self-test questions

1 Name some factors responsible for creating an increase in the demand for new musical compositions.
2 Who was Pietro Metastasio?
3 What is opera seria? Name one opera written in this style by Mozart.
4 Who was the most notable French opera composer of the eighteenth century?
5 Who, or what was La Pouplinière?
6 Name one opera seria written by Handel.
7 Who was Johann Adolf Hasse?
8 What was the name of Pergolesi's most famous comic opera?
9 What was Gluck's significance in the opera world of the eighteenth century?
10 What was English ballad opera? Name one.
11 Name two of the three composers who helped to spread the popularity of Italian opera across Europe.
12 What is the 'claque'?

8

THE NINETEENTH CENTURY

The opera boom

Naming significant composers of opera from the nineteenth century is rather like naming every popular composer you can bring to mind, as well as others who may be unfamiliar to you, and the list would probably take up several pages. Right across Europe, Bohemia, Russia and America, all sorts of composers were trying their hand at opera. To mention just a few who succeeded in Italy alone gives some idea of the scale of work being produced – Donizetti, Bellini, Rossini, Verdi, Puccini, Mascagni and Leoncavallo.

SOUND WORLD NINETEENTH-CENTURY

From approximately the last quarter of the eighteenth century until the end of the nineteenth century, a musical vocabulary was becoming established with its own library of familiar sounds. Successful combinations of instruments had been proven and were used together with what had come to be accepted styles of form, harmony and rhythm.

—— # Nineteenth-century overview ——

The Industrial Revolution, together with a huge rise in population, saw a migration to the cities, and in London and Paris alone the population grew four-fold. This increasingly city-based, impersonal society, where small-community life was no longer possible, bred a desire in artistic circles to recapture the gentle, once familiar pleasures of nature. This ideal was represented in the great landscape paintings of the age, as well as in every other artistic medium.

The Romantic style at this time was viewed as a rebellion against the supposed limitations of the earlier Classical style, but it would be wrong to suppose that every composer attached himself exclusively to Romantic ideals. The world of opera reflects every nuance of opinion throughout the century, and sees as many enormous strides forward as those being accomplished in the areas of science and industry. Altogether, the nineteenth century was one of enormous change. The American Declaration of Independence in 1776, and the French Revolution, which lasted from 1789 until 1794, changed dramatically and forever the needs and aspirations of millions of people. Rather than espousing the cosmopolitan attitudes of the previous century, creative individuals reflected the general mood of increased introspection and the move towards nationalism.

Nationalism

Differences between national styles became increasingly distinct during the nineteenth century. Themes, rhythms, folk song and other traditional music found their way into classical compositions. This freedom, variety and spontaneity held the widest possible appeal, whilst at the same time reflected a particular country's national heritage.

Russia

The Russian musical heritage was especially rich. Traditional folk tunes abounded in a variety that reflected the many different cultures gathered under the vast umbrella of Mother Russia, and church music too was of an extremely high standard, adding more lustre to the mix. The quality of performance generally was high and wealthy families often employed musicians to play in small orchestras or more traditional balalaika groups at their large country estates and elegant town houses. Up and coming composers were beginning to express some dissatisfaction with the fact that, aside from traditional performances, the most fashionable music seemed to be imported from countries whose musical heritage was neither as varied, nor as relevant to Russians as their own.

In the 1730s, the Russian Empress Anna brought Italian opera to court and from this time until around 1840, a succession of Italian composers and singers held sway. Promising Russian musicians and composers were frequently sent to Italy for training and so the preferred style of composition remained stubbornly Italian. By the time of Catherine the Great, who reigned from 1762–96, some Italian trained Russian composers, like Yevstigney Fomin, might use the Russian language, or Russian topics, but the style of their writing had not yet acquired a true national identity. The man who brought about the change was a comfortably off, gifted, though amateur musician, Mikhail Ivanovich Glinka. Returning from travels in Italy, where he absorbed the qualities of Italian opera, and Berlin, where he studied counterpoint, Glinka composed *Life for the Tsar*, now known as *Ivan Susanin*. Combining elements of French and Italian opera with Russian folk song and oriental pastiche, Glinka created a sound world that Russians recognised immediately as the longed for representation of their national identity and culture.

Mikhail Glinka (1804–57)

The 'New Russian School of Music' refers to a nationalistic style of composition that refused to accept the domination of Western 'classical' music. Furthermore, 'classical' training was regarded with scepticism and instead independence of thought and interpretation was encouraged. Glinka was in the vanguard of this movement. He received little formal training, but was well travelled and so in a position to absorb the essence of both French and Italian opera. The individual characteristics of these two forms undoubtedly encouraged him to strive to create a recognisable style for his own nation. Dedicated to the preservation of Russian folk song and to the development of an unique national style. Glinka fulfils these aspirations in his opera *Ivan Susanin*. Folk melodies and the familiar sound of the balalaika are woven into the score and the recitative is written to accord with the inflections of the Russian language.

IVAN SUSANIN

This colourful, essentially Russian opera, was written by Mikhail Glinka (1804–57). Sometimes known as *A life of the Tsar*, the piece resounds to Russian folk tunes and the story is based upon a traditional Russian tale. Staged in St Petersburg in 1836, this opera is considered to be one of the founding musical works of the Russian nationalist movement. (See 'The Five' p 80.)

ALEXANDER DARGOMYZHSKY (1813–1869)

Another Russian from a comfortable background, Dargomy-zhsky imbibed traditional themes from childhood whilst living on his family's country estate. Showing an early gift for music, he was taught piano, violin and composition. His two main operas, *Rusalka* and *The Stone Guest* are notable for their recitative, that whilst melodic, imitates speech tones. This, together with the composer's use of music to create realistic images and his humorous observation of Russian bureaucracy, made him both influential in the field of Russian composition and popular with the public.

The Five

Alexander Borodin (1833–87)
César Cui (1835–1918)
Mily Balakirev (1837–1910)
Modest Mussorgsky (1839–81)
Nikolay Rimsky-Korsakov (1844–1908)

After Glinka's death in 1857, a group of Russian composers came together in St Petersburg to promote national ideals in music. Dubbed 'The Mighty Handful' by their champion, the critic Stassov, the five men rejected Western musican values and set about consolidating a typically Russian style of composition. In Moscow where Western music was highly regarded, they were considered to be eccentric amateurs. They certainly were gentlemen amateurs who learned their craft as they went along, rather than undergoing any form of intensive training, but their place in Russian music is now greatly valued. Together with Balakirev, the founder of the group, was Borodin, a chemist, Cui, a lecturer on fortification at the army Staff college, Mussorgsky, an ex-army officer and Rimsky-Korsakov, an ex-sailor. Of their contributions to opera, Borodin completed only one work, *The Bogatyrs*; Cui wrote seven operas of which *William Ratcliff* was his greatest success and *The Captain's Daughter*, based on a story by Pushkin, his only full-length opera with a Russian theme; Balakirev wrote no opera; Mussorgsky completed one work, his masterpiece of the same name based on Pushkin's *Boris Godunov* and many other unfinished works; Rimsky-Korsakov wrote as many as 16 operas, as well as completing or revising several others by fellow Russians.

Peter Ilich Tchaikovsky (1840–93)

Whilst not insensible to the quality of much of 'the Five's' music, and even prepared upon occasion to compose in the same style himself, Tchaikovsky was critical of their boast that genius flourished where it hadn't been 'trained out of existence.' 'The Mighty Handful' retaliated by naming him after a notorious bandit chief, 'Sadyk-Pasha'.

This friendly rivalry would not prevent the serious-minded Rimsky-Korsakov from seeking technical advice from Tchaikovsky, or Tchaikovsky from infuriating the group all the more by declaring that Russian music was 'tied to the tail of the more cultured Europe'. History has proved that Tchaikovsky, with his gift for depicting human emotion through music, his haunting melodies and his elegant orchestral writing, was the supreme talent in an exceptionally fertile era for Russian music. The stage featured large in Tchaikovsky's life and from the age of 27, he would usually be involved in writing an opera, a ballet, or indeed both. Of his ten operas, two appear as regular inclusions in the repertoire of companies outside Russia; *Eugene Onegin* and *The Queen of Spades*. Tchaikovsky was part-librettist of both works, sharing the writing with Konstantin Shilovsky for *Onegin* and his younger brother, Modest Tchaikovsky, for *The Queen of Spades*. Both works are based on themes by Pushkin, but whereas *The Queen of Spades* is foreshadowed with impending tragedy and has a ghostly element to its love-story, *Eugene Onegin* is a more realistic, though no less hopeless tale of love. By setting this type of intensely personal passionate theme, rather than myth, history or melodrama, Tchaikovsky was able to create the most poignant musical images. In France, composers such as Gounod and Massenet were following the same line.

Charles Gounod (1818–93)

A composer of some 12 operas, Gounod is chiefly remembered for his masterpiece, *Faust*. The theme of sacred and profane love that runs through this work must have had particular significance for a man who, at one time, had been on the point of taking holy orders. Gounod inherited his musical talent from his mother and during his studies at the Paris Conservatoire won the chance to further his studies in church music in Rome. On his return to Paris, he played the organ professionally and also began to study for the priesthood. He enjoyed some success with religious compositions, but then the celebrated mezzo-soprano and some time composer, Pauline Viardot, suggested that he try his hand at opera. Opera, and in particular *Faust*, is certainly the style for which Gounod is chiefly remembered, but he did produce a number of significant religious works. Perhaps the most famous of these is his sacred song, *Ave Maria*, based on Bach's Prelude in C. His oratorios were popular in England, where he was said to be one of Queen Victoria's favourite composers. *Faust* is rich in melody from beginning to end, and this nineteenth century style, with its romantic drama and vivid fantasy element, is best described as **lyric opera**.

Jules Massenet (1842–1912)

Pauline Viardot was also to prove instrumental in furthering the career of this French composer, when she helped to promote his religious musical drama, *Marie-Magdelaine*. The work which really brought his name into prominence however was *Le roi de Lahore* (1877). After the triumph of this opera, Massenet became a much sought after figure and was appointed Professor at the French Conservatoire, where he enjoyed a highly successful teaching career from 1878–96. He was able to combine teaching with composition and of his many operas, two of the most enduringly popular are *Manon* (1884) and *Werther* (1892). With works of this quality and a celebrated teaching career, Massenet was able to enjoy fame in his lifetime.

Bedrich Smetana (1824–84)

It is said that Smetana received his calling as the champion of Czech nationalism, during a gathering of musicians in Weimar at the home of the famous composer and pianist Franz Liszt. Goaded by the Viennese composer Herbeck, who declared that all Bohemia was good for was producing musicians who could play other people's music, Smetana determined to prove him wrong. There was a certain truth in Herbeck's words, since those Czech composers that did exist ploughed a cosmopolitan furrow that did little to reflect their national heritage. Again, Czech musicians in general were admired and much sought after for orchestras and bands, but seemed content to play international music, rather than striving to produce original pieces of their own with a recognisably national flavour. Finally Liszt brought the dispute to an end by playing through the first book of Smetana's character pieces for piano. When he had finished playing, Liszt declared that here at last was a Czech composer with the ability to reflect his country's heritage. Herbeck was so affected by the music that he immediately retracted his statement and shook hands with Smetana. Inspired by the confidence shown to him by his fellow musicians, Smetana determined that henceforth he would dedicate his life to his country and the development of its art. This ambition was fulfilled and Smetana's music became a conduit for the expression of Bohemian patriotism at a time when he and his countrymen were a subject race. His most popular opera is undoubtedly the humourous romp *The Bartered Bride*, which incorporates folk dance and traditional rhythms. Smetana's operas were produced at the National Theatre in Prague where he became principal conductor. In 1874, having suffered nervous and physical disability for some time, Smetana became completely deaf. He continued to compose orchestral works that he would never hear and these together with his works for piano and the stage left a rich catalogue of music not only for the Czech nation, but for the world at large.

ANTONIN DVOŘÁK (1841–1904)

A prominent figure in the nineteenth century nationalist movement, for a time this Czech composer played viola in the orchestra of the National Theatre in Prague which Smetana helped to establish. Between 1866 and 1872, Smetana produced eight works with a national theme, providing the basis of a Czech repertoire in much the same way as Glinka's *LIfe of the Tsar* heralded the start of a recognisably Russian opera tradition. Dvořák added to this catalogue producing another nine operas with a distinct national style between 1872 and 1904; Leoš Jánaček (1854–1928) continued the tradition.

Of all Dvořák's operas, perhaps *Rusalka* or *The Water-Nymph* has enjoyed the most success. The soprano aria, *'Rusalka's song to the moon'* is certainly one of opera's all time favourites and the complete work, like Humperdinck's *Hansel and Gretel*, is popular with children.

Leoš Jánaček (1854–1928)

Another Czech composer who was in tune with the nationalist movement, Jánaček wrote a number of operas, most popular of which have been *Jenufa* and *The Cunning little Vixen*. *Jenufa* is set in a Moravian village and tells a tale of disappointment, murder and deceit, yet manages to have a happy ending. *The Cunning little Vixen* is a comic strip of a tale, detailing the life and death of a fox. It is based on the verses written by Rudolf Tesnohlidek for drawings by Stanislav Lolek. Jánaček was a composer, conductor, teacher and student of his native culture. He studied the inflections of peasant speech and folk song, incorporating these elements in his compositions. Apart from his operas, Jánaček wrote a Slavonic folk mass and several other choral works, together with orchestral and chamber pieces.

ZARZUELA

Zarzuela takes its name from *zarza*, or bramble; the name given to a palace near Madrid which, in the seventeenth century, Philip IV used as a base for hunting and where he also held spectacular entertainments known as *Fiestas de la Zarzuela*. Zarzuela became the name adopted by a certain type of essentially Spanish musical drama. These had a spoken dialogue, could incorporate dance and were usually in a popular style. With themes ranging from tragedy to farce, interplay with the audience was not unknown and plots could be manipulated to allow for topical satirical commentary.

The rapid rise in popularity of Italian opera put a temporary halt to the development of this style in the early part of the eighteenth century, although works by Antonio Literes and Juan de Nebra did achieve success. In the second half of the century, two works written by Antonio Rodriguez de Hita, *Las segadoras de Valleca* (1768) and *Las labradoras de Murcia* (1769) brought about a sustained revival of interest. With the rise of nationalism in the nineteenth century, Zarzuela came into its own and a theatre devoted to this genre was opened in Madrid.

Other notable composers include Juan Hidalgo in the seventeenth century and Franciso Asenjo Barbieri in the nineteenth century. Several composers worked to preserve this style in the twentieth century, including Amadeo Vives (1871–1932) and Jesus Guridi (1886–1961), whose interest in Basque folk music led to his famous Basque Zarzuela, *El caserio* (1926).

—— Classical and Romantic styles ——

Late eighteenth- and early nineteenth-century music is often termed Classical, and music of the rest of the nineteenth century Romantic, but labelling music in an arbitrary fashion like this is full of pitfalls. Given a selection of pieces from the Classical period, there will be some Romantic elements present, and in the Romantic period, elements of the earlier Classical style will be apparent in some compositions.

Carl Maria Friedrich Ernst von Weber (1786–1826)

Yet another composer whose life was cut short, Weber is looked upon as the founder of opera's Romantic school of music. Born near Lübeck in Germany, Weber died from consumption in London at the age of 40.

His father was a travelling actor-manager and Weber's teachers included, in Salzburg Joseph Haydn's younger brother Michael, and in Vienna the Abbé Vogler who also taught Meyerbeer.

Weber succeeded in obtaining musical posts in several minor courts and prior to his marriage, led a rather wild and dissolute life.

In 1813 he was appointed opera director in Prague and set about reforming the sometimes haphazard process of presenting an opera. Interesting himself in every aspect of the production, he also prepared essays, available for all to study, on the works in hand. Singers and musicians were engaged not simply on their musical abilities, but on their skills in ensemble work and ability to work as a team. In 1816 he was engaged by the court in Dresden, where demands on the singers grew.

A more rigorous rehearsal schedule was instituted and texts were read through as a matter of course, establishing the drama in the mind of the performer. In order to improve the blend of sounds, Weber undertook a total reorganisation of singers and musicians, both in seating or standing positions, and in number and classification. His better use of scenery and lighting also helped German opera to take its place on an equal footing with Italian.

In 1821, Weber travelled to Berlin to conduct his own masterpiece, *Der Freischutz*. This example of German Romantic opera enjoyed enormous popularity, which continues to the present day. A Grand opera, *Euryanthe*, met with less success due to a weak libretto, but its music heralds much that was to issue from the pen of Richard Wagner.

Weber's illness was already far advanced when he was invited to compose an opera for the Covent Garden theatre in London. *Oberon* was the result of this commission and, although there are some linking themes that would become usual in Romantic opera, it consisted largely of individual pieces and followed a bizarre plot-line that had more in common with pantomime than with Shakespeare. However, Weber's use of musical characterisation in this opera, notably the fairy music and the storm music, is outstanding and this type of dramatic imagery went on to influence many future composers.

Weber was not satisfied with *Oberon* and had hoped to revise the work to include both recitative and musical links, so that it would more closely represent his notion of a dramatically authentic German style. Sadly he died the day before he was to return to Germany. Gustav Mahler eventually revised *Oberon*, as well as reworking *Euryanthe* and completing a comedy, *Die Drei Pintos*.

A footnote...

Hector Berlioz (1803–69) was certainly one of the most notable composers in the French Romantic style in the nineteenth century (see page 108), but interestingly enough his music was not particularly popular in France. Perhaps his use of great forces in some works, both vocally and in his orchestral writing, did not accord with the French preference for sophistication and subtlety; lyric, rather than epic. Time has shown much of his music to be sincere rather than simple, exhilarating rather than heavy.

Orchestral works such as *Harold in Italy*; *The Roman Carnival*; *Romeo and Juliet* and the oratorio, *The Childhood of Christ*, will certainly prove the point. Berlioz' last years were spent in melancholy solitude and the Shakespearean epitaph he suggested for himself – 'a tale told by an idiot, full of sound and fury, signifying nothing' – does little to reflect a life of music that was to deliver pleasure to so many.

National Society for French Music

This society was formed at the end of the Franco–Prussian war in 1871 with the aim of encouraging French composers to promote a national style. It was hoped that they would derive inspiration not only from traditional French folk melodies, but from music of the past, by composers such as Jean-Philippe Rameau and Christoph Gluck.

Trends in other countries

In Italy, Verdi (see page 144) was certainly a symbol of national unity and in Germany, Wagner (see page 25) stirred nationlistic feelings with his music, yet neither composer's works could be said to have been constrained in any way by nationalist ideals.

In Poland, Stanislaw Moniuszko (1819–72) was responsible for establishing the Polish national opera with his work, *Halka*. In Denmark, Carl August Nielsen (1865–1931) wrote two operas, *Saul og David* (1902) and *Maskarade* is as popular a national opera as is Smetana's *The Bartered Bride*. In Spain, Felipe Pedrell (1841–1922) established a Spanish national style with his trilogy, *Los Pirineos* (1902). Deriving inspiration not only from traditional music and folk song, Pedrell also drew upon a much earlier tradition of Spanish music. He aslo wrote comic opera and Zarzuelas. At this time in America, 'classi-cal' music was still largely imported and in the United Kingdom the first composer to achieve international recognition with music that was particularly 'English' in style, though not derived noticeably from the folk song, was Sir Edward Elgar (1857–1934), who wrote only part of an opera. Intending to be a setting of Barry Jackson's libretto, *The Spanish Lady*, which was taken from Ben Jonson's *The Devil is an Ass*, the work was never completed.

There was a highly successful and particularly English style of music drama generated in the second half of the nineteenth century, that because of its association with the Savoy theatre in London, became known eventually as 'The Savoy Operas'. These witty and tuneful compositions fall into a category of their own and are arguably more closely allied to operetta or the musical style than opera see *Teach Yourself Musicals*. However, if one distinction between opera and the musical is that opera is performed by singers who can act, whereas musicals are performed by actors who can sing, then the light operas of Gilbert and Sullivan still defy easy classification. Some roles demand considerable acting skills and even comic timing, yet many of the principal parts could hardly be said to be simple to sing and cer-tainly require the stamina of a well-trained voice. In most of these operas, there is spoken dialogue, but so there is in *The Magic Flute*. The Savoy operas were written almost to a formula, with principal roles being created for particular individuals, but then roles were created in the same way by some of the most highly renowned opera composers. William Schwenck Gilbert's brilliant satirical pieces, together with Arthur Sullivan's catchy melodies and exhilarating, if predictable, rhythms, gave the Victorian public an often humorous, certainly stylised and unquestionably chaste, entertainment which they took to their hearts.

The strength of Gilbert's scripts and libretti is emphasised by the fact that he eventually gained equal billing with Sullivan. However, the partnership might not have enjoyed the same success without one more ingredient: the impresario, Richard D'Oyly Carte. Some-time composer, theatrical manager and artistes agent, 'Oily Carte' as he was dubbed for his shrewdness, realised that he did not possess suffi-cient talent to forge a career for himself as a musician, but proceeded to show the greatest facility in nurturing and promoting the musical careers of others. He was also keen to establish an English operatic tradition. The rest as they say, is history...

The nineteenth century: self-test questions

1 Name three Italian composers who came to prominence in the nineteenth century.
2 What was one cause of people migrating to the cities?
3 What elements did nationalism bring into a country's music?
4 What is Zarzuela?
5 Who was known as the founder of Romantic opera?
6 Name one opera written by Carl Weber.
7 Name some ways in which Weber achieved a better balance of sound in performance.
8 Who were 'The Five'?
9 Name one opera written by Mikhail Glinka.
10 Name one opera written by Tchaikovsky.
11 Name Gounod's most famous sacred song.
12 What nationality was Bedrich Smetana?

9
THE TWENTIETH CENTURY

The twentieth century has been a busy time for opera. There might seem to be an unfathomable gulf between the melodic lushness of Puccini and the sensory and cerebral challenges of an opera by Birtwhistle, but like progress in scientific and social areas, developments in music have also raced ahead at an unprecedented rate. With the advent of electronic instruments and amplification, new techniques have become increasingly available. No one style is mandatory, but elements of many different idioms offer twentieth-century composers the widest possible stimulus. National styles and folk idioms have continued to prosper, while in the works of composers such as Arnold Schoenberg, his pupil Alban Berg, and the self-taught Austrian composer Josef Hauer, boundaries have been pushed out further still, to embrace exciting new experiments in sound. Atonality, together with a variety of other approaches to the ordering of musical notes, has challenged the public's conception of what to expect from a night at the opera. Other leanings, towards the classicism of the past, to impressionism, or to evocative themes and exoticism have also thrived and each of these elements may predominate, or coexist happily in twentieth-century compositions.

Some contemporary works are challenged for being derivative, or pastiche, but history shows that even composers such as Mozart have not been wholly blameless when it comes to occasional poaching. Other modern works, dismissed by some as noisome rubbish, join a whole host of now popular operas in being received at their inception with negative reactions. History will be the final judge of what will and will not survive and what will and will not be the most significant landmarks in the development of opera in the twentieth century.

Because this has been a century of such immense diversification, it is impossible to resist taking a brief look at some composers who have made a significant contribution to that variety. After all, you may find just what you're looking for 'off the beaten track'. This last, but certainly not final, part of the history of opera reveals some unusual styles, so that in total you can see what a wealth of interpretations has developed over the 300 years or more since the Florentine Camerata first met. The very fact that opera remains a subject of lively debate and myriad interpretation ensures not just its survival, but its guaranteed evolution into the next century and beyond.

Richard Strauss (1864–1949)

This post-Romantic German composer should not be confused with members of the Viennese Strauss family. In 1905 after two previous operas, *Guntram* and *Feuersnot*, Strauss had his first really big success with the one act opera *Salome*. The orchestral music is so dominant that the work has been described as an orchestral 'tone poem' with added vocal parts. Strauss was a famous conductor by the time *Salome* was staged, and is famously said to have ordered the orchestra to play louder as he could still hear the singers. *Salome*'s theme scandalised the public, yet its brazen music served to place Strauss at the head of the avant-garde movement. In 1909, his opera *Electra* also shocked with an even more radical musical style. *Electra* is based on a play by Sophocles and benefits from Strauss's partnership with the librettist Hugo von Hofmannsthal. This alliance would prove extremely fruitful, and in *Electra* Hofmannsthal displays a deft touch, moving away from the horror and darkness to stress the human tragedy instead. Strauss brings the libretto to life with musical dissonances, unexpected harmonic progressions and some of the most distinct musical characterisation to be found in his work to date. By contrast, the opera *Der Rosenkavalier* is a delightful *mélange* of passion, humour and love set in eighteenth century Vienna. This collaboration with Hoffmannsthal captures the effortless sophistication in aristocratic circles at the time and, together with his symphonic poem *Till Eulenspiegel*, provides arguably the most enjoyably melodic of all his compositions. There would be more operas (see page 121) as well as a good deal of instrumental music and many songs.

A clutch of British composers added lustre to twentieth century opera tradition in the UK, amongst whom were:

Ralph Vaughan Williams (1872–1958)

Enjoying a formal education at Charterhouse, Cambridge and finally the Royal College of Music, Vaughan Williams was to become the foremost British composer at the beginning of the twentieth century. An avid collector and student of folk song, he combined these national elements with the musical ideas of his classical training. His compositions ranged from hymn tunes to operas and he was also keen to produce music suitable for amateur performance, for instance *Benedicte* (1930) and *Household music* (1941). As well as his quintessentially English operas, songs such as *Linden Lea* have enjoyed lasting success as have his several choral works. Music for the film *Scott of the Antarctic*, and orchestral works such as *Fantasia on a Theme of Tallis* are further examples of his diversity, and the incidental music to *The Wasps* is humorous and fun. The music of Vaughan Williams is lyrical and evocative and will certainly repay further investigation.

Gustav Holst (1874–1934)

A friend of Vaughan Williams, Gustav Holst is possibly best remembered for his orchestral suite *The Planets*. Undoubtedly one of the most entertaining and popular works in the classical repertoire, the enormous success of *The Planets* has almost certainly eclipsed Holst's other works, and in particular his operas *The Perfect Fool* and *At the Boar's Head*.

Said to be born with a pen in his hand ready to compose music and eager to learn how to play every instrument that came his way, Holst was fortunate indeed to have Charles Villiers Stanford as his tutor in composition at the Royal College of Music. Influenced both by folk song and by Hindu mysticism, Holst's music is rich in variety which is nowhere better evidenced than in his *Planets* suite. During the First World War, Holst offered his services to the British forces and engendered an enormous and totally unexpected amount of enthusiasm for music amongst the troops in both Salonica and Constantinople. Huge consignments of music books were sent for, together with a large number of copies for Byrd's *Three Part Mass*, unquestionable proof of Holst's success in sharing his love of music with as many people as possible and in whatever circumstances.

William Walton (1902–83)

Born in Oldham and largely self taught, Walton was knighted in 1951 and received the Order of Merit for his services to music in 1968. Apart from his operas *Troilus and Cressida* and the short one-act opera *The Bear*, there were outstanding orchestral works, chamber music, songs and a wonderfully dramatic piece for baritone, chorus and orchestra, *Belshazzar's Feast*. His music for the film *Henry V* is remarkable and the sophisticated and witty entertainment *Facade* is a must for any CD collection. In *Facade* Walton's music forms the most perfect partnership for Dame Edith Sitwell's piquant poems. Walton met the Sitwells at Oxford and was drawn towards and then within their rather eccentric 'arty' circle. However, the boy from Oldham with his musical genius was more than a match for the many exceptional people he would meet through his assocation with the Sitwells.

Michael Tippet (b. 1905)

Sir Michael Tippet was knighted in 1966, having received the CBE for his services to music in 1959. Born in London and trained at the Royal College of Music, his operas are amongst the most important contributions to British opera in the twentieth century. Combining contemporary and classical elements with great facility, both in his style of composition and in his use of traditional and modern instruments, Tippett produces works that are at once thought provoking and entertaining. An additional strength of his work is that, by writing his own lyrics, he forges a close bond between musical and verbal expression. His oratorio *A Child of our Time* will also repay investigation.

Benjamin Britten (1913–76)

Lord Britten of Aldeburgh, as he would become in later life, won a scholarship to the Royal College of Music, where he studied with the composers Frank Bridge and John Ireland. Like them, Britten would write many songs including the haunting *Fish on the Unruffled Lakes* and powerful song cycles such as *On this Island*. Britten is one of the most prolific composers of the twentieth century and his choral works are an area of particular note: works such as *A Boy was Born*, *A Ceremony of Carols* and the *War Requiem* are certainly worth having in a CD collection. The *War Requiem* is enriched by the poems of Wilfred Owen, which include poignant observations of war by this young English soldier who was killed in France in 1918.

Britten's operas reflect his keen sense of the dramatic and enjoy a large following. *Peter Grimes* created a sensation when it was staged in 1945 and proved beyond doubt that the English operatic tradition was firmly established. Britten's versatility and imagination is amply apparent in works such as *Let's Make an Opera* and *The Little Sweep*; the former shows a group of adults and children rehearsing for a performance of *The Little Sweep*.

Noyes Fludde calls upon adults and children, both professional and amateur, and demonstrates Britten's skill at combining performers of varied ability to the greatest effect. Film music and incidental music add to his vast catalogue of compositions and when he was commissioned by the BBC to write an opera for television. *Owen Wingrave* proved that Britten could make every medium his own. In 1948 Benjamin Britten, together with the tenor Peter Pears, founded a festival at Aldeburgh. Apart from establishing a forum where contemporary composers, poets and playwrights could come together to create new works, Aldeburgh also provided Britten with the opportunity to conduct, not just his own works but others in the repertory of the English Opera Group. This group was formed in 1947 by Britten, John Piper and Eric Crozier and would draw upon some of the finest available artistes. Aldeburgh became renowned for the quality of its performances, which drew upon composers such as Mozart, Berkeley and Birtwistle as well as Britten.

Arnold Schoenberg (1874–1951)

This Austrian composer employed devices other than melody to convey his operas' message. *Erwartung*, or *Expectation*, was written in 1909 and first staged in Prague in 1924. As an example of Expressionism in music, the theme is concerned with the inner workings of the mind. *Erwartung* was one of the first operas to discard the usual Western system of chords, scales, or in other words, the type of sounds people were accustomed to hearing. Written in 17 days, this work traces the reactions of a woman searching for, and then discovering, the dead body of her lost lover. Schoenberg's second opera, *Die glückliche Hand*, uses a similar technique to expand its theme, and the main character's quest for truth is not so dissimilar to the ideals explored in the operas of Richard Wagner. A third opera, *Von Heute auf Morgen*, uses 12-note serialist principles for the first time. Serialism takes away the composer's free will and ties the composition to a pre-ordained set of sounds and rules. Schoenberg completed three operas, but a fourth, the unfinished *Moses and Aaron*, was staged in 1957 in Zurich.

Again delving deep into the human psyche, *Moses and Aaron* is perhaps the most readily accessible of Schoenberg's operas. Points of contrast, fusion and compromise between God's message as received by Moses and God's message as relayed by Aaron are reflected clearly in the music, as some more familiar sounds are woven into the new musical vision.

Igor Stravinsky (1882–1971)

Not to be confused with his father the famous Russian Bass, Fyodor Stravinsky, Igor Stravinsky has bequeathed to the world a wealth of exciting and passionate music. At first he intended to be a lawyer, but it was during a trip to Germany that Stravinsky met the composer Rimsky-Korsakov and his future was decided. A subsequent meeting with Diaghilef caused him to settle in Paris, and a series of scores for the ballet followed. Stravinsky's works could sometimes experience several incarnations, for instance his opera *The Nightingale* provided parts which were used to form a symphonic poem (a term used to describe a short, evocative orchestral piece in the Romantic style), and then out of this Stravinsky created a ballet. Becoming a French citizen in 1934, Stravinsky then moved to the United States during the Second World War and was naturalised there in 1945. He experimented with various effects and styles in his operas, for instance in *Oedipus rex* masks are worn by the singers, both to convey a sense of impending tragedy and to complement the choice of Latin, a dead language, for the libretto. The last of his eight operas, *The Rake's Progress*, with its text by W. H. Auden and Chester Kallman, was based on eight engravings by Hogarth and premiered in Venice in 1951. In 1975, a fresh interpretation was produced by John Cox and staged at Glyndebourne, with an exuberant set design by the Bradford artist David Hockney.

Sergey Prokofiev (1891–1953)

Another pupil of Rimsky-Korsakov, this brilliant Russian pianist and composer brought both humour and passion into his work. After the Russian revolution, Prokofiev left for the United States where his opera *The Love of the Three Oranges* was to be staged in Chicago in 1921. With a Russian libretto, taken by the composer from Carlo Gozzi's comedy of 1761, this work allowed for some broad characterisation at which Prokofiev excelled. His career path was not as smooth as might have been expected, and he went back to Paris, returning to the States only for the opera's premiere. In 1936, he returned to Russia, where the repressive political climate was, for a time, partly ameliorated by his hero's welcome. In 1948 however, his opera *War and Peace* was judged to be at fault by a tribunal drawn up to consider the appropriateness, or not, of a number of Russian compositions. Prokofiev promised to review his musical language in the light of these criticisms and this led to the eventual acceptance of the work, which was even chosen to open the season at the Bolshoi Theatre. With over a dozen operas to his credit, together with his orchestral works, film scores, ballets, numerous compositions for the piano and his works for children, including the enduringly delightful *Peter and the Wolf*, Sergey Prokofiev is a composer who will more than repay further investigation.

Darius Milhaud (1892–1974)

Born in Aix-en-Provence in France, Darius Milhaud was one of the 'Group of Six' French composers, credited with bringing about a renaissance of French music through their unified aims, one of which was a return to simplicity. The other members of the group were Louis Durey (1888–1979), Arthur Honegger (1892–1955), Germaine Tailleferre (1892–1983), Georges Auric (1899–1983) and Francis Poulenc (1899–1963). Interestingly enough, like the Florentine Camerata before them, this Group of Six like-minded musicians also met for some time on a regular basis. On Saturday evenings cocktails followed by dinner and sometimes a visit to the fair at Montmartre, or the Cirque Medrano, would fuel the late-night soirées back at Milhaud's home, when recent compositions of the group would be aired and commented upon. Not surprisingly, strains of the music hall, jazz, folksong and other popular idioms can be detected in many of the resulting compositions.

Milhaud flirted with an idea first proposed by Erik Satie (1866–1925), in which 'background' music was to be created. Satie's original idea was that this type of music should enhance surroundings in the same way that a beautiful picture might, but that it should not demand complete attention all the time. This was never wholly successful, since music written for such a purpose by these musicians could never hope to accomplish the vanishing trick of later, mass-produced 'muzak'.

Another device with which Milhaud experimented was the composition of musical parts in more than one key, or home tonality, known as 'Polytonality'. This was not an original idea, since Bach had used this same device in his keyboard music in the early eighteenth century. A setting of *La mère coupable*, the third play in Beaumarchais' *Figaro* trilogy, three 'mini-operas' lasting no more than 15 minutes, contrasting with the epic *Christophe Colomb*, plus a collaboration with Jean Cocteau on *Le pauvre matelot*, gives just a flavour of the variety of work produced by Milhaud. Following a fairly conventional path, in which the voice was featured rather than the orchestra together with a recognisable form, means that Milhaud can be said to possess a distinctive style that draws upon past traditions.

Carl Orff (1895–1982)

This German composer produced a rich catalogue of work. Benefiting from a thorough musical education, including the study of early music, Carl Orff went on to co-found, with Dorothee Gunther, the

Gunther School in Munich. Expression and rhythmical training was encouraged through dance, and Carl Orff's compositions enhanced this process. One of his most exciting works, *Carmina Burana*, cannot truly be called an opera, since it can only be part staged as tableaux, rather than a succession of dramatic scenes. Nevertheless, the music and atmosphere created by the work is riveting. Using ribald rhymes and primitive rhythms, overlaid with ecclesiastical plainsong, folk-song and strains of an earlier time, this work is a 'must have' in any record collection. His operas have not achieved the widespread popularity of *Carmina Burana*, and of these, *Die Kluge*, first staged in Frankfurt in 1943, is possibly the most successful.

John Cage (b. 1912)

It is possible to say that the American John Cage has never composed an opera; there again, it is possible to say that John Cage has created circumstances out of which an opera might develop. In his work *Variations IV*, any number of performers and musicians may produce any number of sounds, in any combination or order, by any means and with or without other activities. These other activities might include dance, drama, singing, or simply the preservation of silence. Chaos? Certainly not! It's 'do-it-yourself opera'.

Philip Glass (b. 1912)

This American composer is associated with the Minimalist school of music. In other words, less is more. His four-act opera *Einstein on the beach* contains four 'knee plays', so called because the knee joins other parts. Three different images contained within these scenes prompt the characters to sing or speak words that have no connection whatever with anything. Numbers are repeated at random, for instance, but the composer is seeking your subjective response to his particular type of 'music theatre', rather than expecting you to form any objective impressions.

———————— Into the future ————————

Improvisation, that singers' delight of the sixteenth century, is being actively encouraged by some modern composers. In the works of John

Cage, for example, the performers are supposed to take a full part in the creative process, and so the wheel comes full circle.

The means to make an accurate sound and picture record of ethnic music, together with a vast library of electronic sounds, has widened the palette of possibilities for today's composers beyond reckoning. What would Mozart or Monteverdi have made of such resources? We can only wonder, and then guess which of the modern composers might have the ability to enrich the lives of future generations. With such a variety of music for you to choose from, the time has come to begin selecting and discarding. Be confident, because I can assure you that somewhere out there, there is definitely a style to suit you.

The twentieth century: self-test questions

1 Name at least two composers who have experimented with new sound worlds in the twentieth century.
2 Explain the term Expressionism as found in twentieth-century compositions. Give one example of such a work.
3 How does serialism affect the composer?
4 Name the opera by Igor Stravinsky in which the singers usually wear masks.
5 Who designed the sets for the 1975 production at Glyndebourne of Stravinsky's *The Rake's Progress*?
6 Name one popular opera by Sergey Prokofiev.
7 By what name was the group of French composers to which Darius Milhaud belonged known?
8 What similarities were there between this group and the Florentine Camerata?
9 Who wrote *Carmina Burana*?
10 What may the performers do in John Cage's work *Variations IV*?
11 Which American composer is associated with the Minimalist school of music?

SUMMARY OF
NOTABLE OPERAS

1597	*Daphne*	Jacopo Peri
1600	*Euridice*	Jacopo Peri
1607	*Orpheus*	Claudio Monteverdi
1627	*Daphne*	Heinrich Schutz
1671	*Pomone*	Robert Camert
1689	*Dido and Aeneas*	Henry Purcell
1711	*Rinaldo*	George Frederic Handel
1733	*La Serva Padrone*	Giovanni Pergolese
1737	*Castor and Pollux*	Jean-Philippe Rameau
1762	*Artaxerxes*	Thomas Arne
1767	*Apollo et Hyacinthus*	Wolfgang Amadeus Mozart
1792	*Il Matrimonio Secreto*	Domenico Cimarosa
1794	*Tammany*	James Hewitt
1805	*Fidelio*	Ludwig van Beethoven
1816	*The Barber of Seville*	Gioacchino Antonio Rossini
1821	*Der Freischutz*	Carl Maria von Weber
1830	*Anna Bolena*	Gaetano Donizetti
1831	*La Sonnambula*	Vincenzo Bellini
1831	*Robert the Devil*	Giacomo Meyerbeer
1836	*A Life for the Czar*	Michael Glinka
1842	*Rienzi*	Richard Wagner
1843	*The Bohemian Girl*	Michael Balfe
1844	*Ernani*	Giuseppe Verdi
1858	*Orpheus in the Underworld*	Jacques Offenbach
1859	*Faust*	Charles François Gounod
1863	*The Trojans at Carthage*	Hector Berlioz

1866	*The Bartered Bride*	Frederick Smetana
1868	*Cox and Box*	Arthur Sullivan
1873	*Ivan the Terrible*	Nikolay Rimsky-Korsakov
1874	*Boris Godunof*	Modeste Mussorgsky
1874	*Die Fledermaus*	Johann Strauss the second
1875	*Carmen*	Georges Bizet
1875	*Trial by Jury*	Gilbert and Sullivan
1877	*Samson and Delilah*	Charles Saint-Saens
1879	*Eugene Onegin*	Peter Tchaikovsky
1883	*Lakmé*	Clement Delibes
1884	*Manon*	Jules Massenet
1890	*Cavalleria Rusticana*	Pietro Mascagni
1890	*Prince Igor*	Alexander Borodin
1892	*I Pagliacci*	Ruggiero Leoncavallo
1893	*Hansel and Gretel*	Engelbert Humperdinck
1893	*Manon Lescaut*	Giacomo Puccini
1894	*Guntram*	Richard Strauss
1896	*Andrea Chénier*	Umberto Giodarno
1900	*Louise*	Gustave Charpentier
1901	*Russalka*	Antonin Dvorak
1902	*Adriana Lecouvreur*	Francesco Cilea
1902	*Pelléas et Mélisande*	Claude Debussy
1904	*Irmelin*	Frederick Delius
1922	*Opera Ala Afro American*	George Gershwin
1924	*Hugh the Drover*	Ralph Vaughan Williams
1925	*Wozzeck*	Alban Berg
1926	*Der Protagonist*	Kurt Weill
1945	*Peter Grimes*	Benjamin Britten
1951	*Amahl and the Night Visitor*	Gian Carlo Menotti
1954	*Tender Land*	Aaron Copland
1955	*Troilus and Cressida*	William Walton
1955	*The Midsummer Marriage*	Michael Tippett
1957	*West Side Story*	Leonard Bernstein
1968	*Punch and Judy*	Harrison Birtwhistle

NOTABLE OPERAS
THROUGH THE AGES

Tens of thousands of operas are known and recorded, but this table lists those whose continuing significance helps to explains the development of opera.

Sixteenth century – the birth of opera

1597   *Daphne* by Jacopo Peri (1561–1633)
       First performance in Florence. All the music, apart from two fragments which were written by Jacopo Corsi, is now lost. 'Reciting' style, whereby a drama was intoned to musical notes with the performer expressing every emotion and thought through the medium of music, preceded opera. Peri went further, developing the melodious content of the reciting, or recitative. As both composer and performer, he was able to combine his skills to give full weight to the expression of the words and realisation of the music. All Italy was said to express delight at his performance in this opera. Forty years later, Monteverdi developed what was to become known as the Florentine style further still, and would describe the correct manner of singing it as 'sung to the time of the heart's feeling and not to that of the hand'.

Seventeenth century – opera style awakes in Germany, France and England

1600   *Euridice* by Jacopo Peri
       Some parts of *Euridice* were written by a fellow singer and

composer, Giulio Caccini. Caccini is said to have written the best 'tunes', whereas Peri's talent lay in conveying the drama. This is the first opera, based upon a secular theme, to have survived intact. Success led it to be performed in Florence, at the wedding of Queen Maria de Medici, where Peri's popularity was reaffirmed. Accompanying instruments would have included lutes and a harpsichord.

1607   *Orpheus* by Claudio Monteverdi (1567–1643)
A pivotal figure in the development of opera, Monteverdi extended the scope of the recitative line and added orchestral interludes, arias, duets and ensemble work, together with dances. The orchestra might now number as many as 40 instruments, including flutes, trumpets, cornetts, sackbuts, string instruments, harpsichord and wooden pipe organ. This work was first performed during the carnival season in Mantua to honour the young prince Francesco Gonzaga.

1627   *Daphne* by Heinrich Schutz (1585–1672)
First German opera and an adaptation of Peri's *Daphne*. Having studied in Venice with Giovanni Gabrieli, Schutz helped to spread the operatic style to northern Europe. Considered the greatest German composer of the early seventeenth century, Schutz's renown now rests largely on his religious works, the most famous being, in oratorio style, *The Seven Last Words*.

1671   *Pomone* by Robert Cambert (1628–77)
First French opera. The French considered their theatrical presentations, in which music was incidental to the drama, greatly superior to what they saw as the exaggerations of the Italian style. Eventually, the strong traditions of ballet and classical tragedy as represented by Pierre Corneille and Jean Racine, gave the French a means of making opera their own. *Pomone* was an immediate success when it became the opening presentation at the Académie Royale des Opera. Cambert had been instrumental in turning the building into a theatre and it would become the first home of the Paris Opera.

1673   *Cadmus et Hermione* by Jean-Baptiste Lully (1632–87)
This French composer of Italian birth set the standard by which French opera would be judged up to, and in certain cases, beyond the French revolution. Lully took an active interest in all aspects of production, as well as the shaping of the libretti for his operas. First performed in Paris in 1673,

this work's appeal spread beyond France, and a performance was given in London in 1686. Lully is generally considered to be the leading French composer of his generation.

1689 *Dido and Aeneas* by Henry Purcell (1658–95)

The first English opera. Purcell was an intensely gifted and prolific composer, whose tragically foreshortened life was a great loss to English music. Melodies such as *Dido's lament* possess the same power to move now as they did 300 years ago. Considered a major work by any standards, this opera is actually a miniature gem, having been composed for a girl's boarding school in Chelsea. Not surprisingly, the chorus is an important element of the piece. There are four principal roles and although there are three acts, the complete work takes only about an hour to perform. The orchestration is straightforward, consisting of strings and harpsichord.

Eighteenth century – the great awakening

Many more operas are written and some of the most notable composers make their debut . . .

1711 *Rinaldo* by George Frederic Handel (1685–1759)

A German by birth, Handel became a British subject in 1726. He is considered to be the greatest composer of opera in the late Baroque period. The aria *Cara Sposa* from *Rinaldo* is a perfect example of his expressive writing. Whilst on leave from his post in Hanover, Handel spotted the opportunity for a composer of significance to fill the operatic void in London. A businessman as well as musician, Handel produced *Rinaldo* quickly, incorporating previous compositions in the race to finish the work before his return to Hanover. This opera may have been conceived in a calculating manner, but it clearly shows the skill, variety and excellence of its composer's work.

1733 *La Serva Padrone* by Giovanni Battista Pergolesi (1710–36)

Pergolese died aged only 26, yet achieved great renown. His major works included no fewer than 15 operas and 12 cantatas. *La Serva Padrone* is a light-hearted romp, considered to be one of the first great examples of opera buffa. The significance of this opera lies in the fact that the characters typified real people in contemporary dress, rather than exaggerated 'classical' heroes and heroines, or gods and goddesses. The premiere of this work was greeted enthusiastically, and its popularity has never waned.

1737   *Castor and Pollux* by Jean-Philippe Rameau (1683–1764)

A founder of musical theory as we know it today, Rameau came to fame in his fifties. This opera is considered to be his masterpiece, but despite making such a significant contribution to the development of opera in Europe, Rameau was no stranger to controversy. His operas aroused strong feelings, both from admirers and from those who saw him as a subverter of the traditional French operatic style as represented by Lully.

1762   *Artaxerxes* by Thomas Arne (1710–78)

Best remembered for *Rule Britannia*, Arne was a noteworthy British composer whose tunes are timeless. Musically in the 'Italian' style, but sung in English, this opera enjoyed great success and was the first example of opera seria to enjoy lasting fame.

1762   *Orpheus and Euridice* by Christoph Willibald Gluck (1714–87)

Born in Bavaria, Gluck's main operatic works were composed in Vienna, with some lesser operas written in Paris. A friend of Handel, he is now considered by some to be a forerunner of Wagner. This opera was the first example of the composer's so-called 'reform' operas. It combines song, dance, recitative and a more sophisticated orchestration than before. Expressive qualities make this early classicial opera a real pleasure to listen to. *Che faro, senza Euridice?* is one of the most memorable melodies.

1767   *Apollo et Hyacinthus* by Wolfgang Amadeus Mozart (1756–91)

Composed as an Intermezzo, this mini-opera was performed between the acts of a play celebrating the end of the university year in Salzburg. In the style of opera seria, this was Mozart's first staged opera.

1792   *Il matrimonio secreto* by Domenico Cimarosa (1749–1801)

Salieri's successor as Kapellmeister in Vienna, the Italian Cimarosa, wrote more than 60 operas. Though none of his operas survive as regular inclusions in the modern repertoire, Cimarosa is regarded as a most important figure in the development of operatic style, due to his skilled use of drama, appealing melodies and inspired ensemble writing. When this opera was first performed at the Imperial court in Vienna, it was so well received that the encore involved the repetition of the whole piece, earning the cast a free supper.

1794   *Tammany* by James Hewitt (1770–1827)
An American composer of English birth. The first American opera, produced in New York, where James Hewitt was the conductor at the Park Street Theatre.

Nineteenth century – the great opera bulge

1805   *Fidelio* by Ludwig van Beethoven (1770–1827)
One of the greatest and most prolific of all German composers, Beethoven wrote only one opera, yet that single work placed him amongst the foremost composers of the style. Unsuccessful at its premiere in 1805, it took two revisions before the final version of 1814 earned lasting acclaim.

1816   *The Barber of Seville* by Gioacchino Antonio Rossini (1792–1868)
One of the best-loved works of all time – though hissed at its first performance!

1821   *Der Freischutz* by Carl Maria von Weber (1786–1826)
A great German nationalist, Weber is thought of as the founder of the Romantic school of opera, where the rousing of emotions took precedence over all else. This, Weber's fifth performed opera, earned him the widest acclaim with its celebration of German folklore and wonderful music.

1830   *Anna Bolena* by Gaetano Donizetti (1797–1848)
Premiered in Milan, Donizetti's first 'tragic' opera won international acclaim. One of the most prolific opera composers ever, Donizetti may be considered a forerunner of another great composer of operas, Giuseppe Verdi.

1831   *La Sonnambula* by Vincenzo Bellini (1801–35)
A significant contributor to Italian opera, Bellini's vocal writing allows the singers every opportunity to display their vocal prowess. This, Bellini's seventh opera, was a huge success on its first night at the Teatro Carcano, Milan. Slow to capitalise on its success in Italy, *Sonnambula* became a great favourite of Victorian audiences in England. It enjoyed a great revival in 1957, when the outstanding soprano Maria Callas made the part of Amina her own.

1831   *Robert the Devil* by Giacomo Meyerbeer (1791–1864)

Famed initially as a piano virtuoso, Meyerbeer used expert orchestral writing, lavish staging and the finest singers of the day to put the Grand into Grand Opera. This work together with another by the same composer, *Les Huguenots*, helped establish and popularise the style.

1836   *A Life for the Czar* by Michael Glinka (1804–57)

Brought up on a country estate in Russia, Glinka travelled to Italy as an adult, where he met Donizetti, and Bellini. This opera, premiered in St Petersburg, is as lyrical as an Italian opera, yet with the unmistakably nationalistic strains that would mark its composer, together with Alexander Dargomijsky, as a forerunner of the famous 'group of Five'. The Five, as they were known, were Mily Balikirev (1837–1910), César Cui (1835–1918), Alexander Borodin (1833–87), Modeste Mussorgsky (1839–81) and Nikolay Rimsky-Korsakov (1844–1908). All of these shared the same Russian nationalist sentiments, which were represented to varying degrees in their music. Interestingly enough, none of the Five was primarily a musician, but came from a comfortable background and varied professions.

It is significant that in the nineteenth century, with the advent of nationalism, composers of opera in several countries, and Russia in particular, shook off many elements of Italian influence.

1839   *Oberto* by Giuseppe Verdi (1813–1901)

The earliest opera by Verdi to have survived. *Oberto* is thought to contain some material from this composer's first completed opera (1836) *Rocester*, which is now lost. *Oberto* was completed when Verdi was in his twenties. His last opera, *Falstaff*, was staged in Milan in his eightieth year, 1893.

1842   *Rienzi* by Richard Wagner (1813–83)

The appearance of Wagner as opera composer, rather than the opera itself, is the particular landmark in this case. Wagner wrote his own scripts, or libretti, and used the idea of a theme, or *leitmotiv*, to represent certain characters or emotions. With this tool he was able to strengthen the effect of the drama upon his audience. Wagner based *Rienzi*'s libretto on a drama by Mary Russell Mitford and a novel by Bulwer Lytton. Set in fourteenth-century Rome and containing plenty of violence and heroism, this five-act opera premiered in Dresden.

1843   *The Bohemian Girl* by Michael Balfe (1808–70)
An Irishman, living in England, Balfe began his career as an opera singer, then went into business for himself, producing his own opera on the London stage, with his wife in the leading role.

1858   *Orpheus in the Underworld* by Jacques Offenbach (1819–90)
Strictly speaking an operetta (see Glossary) this work was enormously successful, making its composer famous throughout France, other parts of Europe and the United States.

1859   *Faust* by Charles François Gounod (1818–93)
Successfully premiered in Paris, this opera is full of memorable tunes and has an engaging play, loosely based on Goethe's drama of the same name. *The Soldiers' chorus*, which was actually extracted from an earlier, unsuccessful work, *Ivan the Terrible*, is an all-time favourite piece.

1863   *The Trojans at Carthage* by Hector Berlioz (1803–69)
Based upon Virgil's *Aenid* and premiered in Paris, this enormous undertaking was split into two parts with the first part of the drama, *The Capture of Troy*, staged in Karlsruhe in 1890, long after the composer's death. On completing the epic, Berlioz is said to have remarked that he wrote his comedy *Beatrice and Benedict* just to take a rest! A dramatic composer and true Romantic, in both the artistic and literal sense, Hector Berlioz made a significant contribution to French music.

1866   *The Bartered Bride* by Frederick Smetana (1824–84)
Smetana was a champion of the nationalist cause in his native Bohemia. His humourous opera, which premiered in Prague, bore all the hallmarks of nationalism, both in its musical and dramatic content. Representing national pride to the Czech people, Smetana ended his life sadly in an asylum suffering from deafness and syphilis.

1867   *Cox and Box* by Arthur Sullivan (1842–1900)
Sir Arthur Sullivan was one half of the great 'double act' Gilbert and Sullivan, who together with the impresario Sir Richard D'Oyly Carte, created the English phenomenon known collectively as the Savoy Operas. Sullivan wrote the one-act farce *Cox and Box* together with an earlier collaborator, the librettist, F. C. Burnand.

1873　*Ivan the Terrible* [otherwise known as *The Maid of Pskov* or *Pskovitianka*] by Nikolay Rimsky-Korsakov (1844–1908)
A great nationalist, all but two of this composer's operas took Russian themes. Rhythm, folk tunes and a vivid use of orchestral scoring, typify this composer's work, although of his many operas only *The Golden Cockerel* enjoys much popularity outside Russia.

1874　*Boris Godunof* by Modeste Mussorgsky (1839–81)
Another Russian nationalist, Mussorgsky's operas enjoyed little success during his lifetime and his most popular work inside Russia, *Boris Godunof*, was 'improved' by Rimsky-Korsakov. Today Mussorgsky's original version is valued as a great work by the Russian people, and his interpretation is the one most usually performed.

1874　*Die Fledermaus* by Johann Strauss the second (1825–99)
The eldest son of Johann Strauss the first, Johann Strauss the second continued the great Viennese tradition of melody and sophistication. Strictly speaking an operetta, *Die Fledermaus* provides a rich feast of good tunes, colourful drama and light-hearted entertainment.

1875　*Carmen* by Georges Bizet (1838–75)
Bizet didn't live to enjoy the success of his operas, in particular *Carmen*. A more powerful drama than his other, still-popular works, *The Pearl Fishers* and *The Fair Maid of Perth*, *Carmen* enjoys an enduring and justly deserved popularity. Although French by birth and choice, all, with the possible exception of Spaniards themselves, feel that Bizet captured the rhythms and passions of Spain and transferred them successfully to the stage.

1875　*Trial by Jury* by Gilbert and Sullivan
The first theatrical collaboration of Sir William Schwenk Gilbert (1836–1911) and Arthur Sullivan. These two formed a true partnership, where the satirical libretti of Gilbert were as crucial to the whole as was Sullivan's music.

1877　*Samson and Delilah* by Charles Camille Saint-Saëns (1835–1921)
An author, child prodigy on the piano and prolific composer, Saint Saëns was also a great champion of early French composers. Out of 13 operas written by this composer, only *Samson and Delilah* survives in the regular operatic repertoire. Initially banned from Paris due to its biblical references,

the opera premiered in Weimar. A sustained, emotional story-line, together with strong melodies ensures its lasting popularity.

1879   *Eugene Onegin* by Peter Ilich Tchaikovsky (1840–93)

Tchaikovsky possessed an appeal that transcended national boundaries and made him the first truly popular Russian composer. He wrote ten operas and declared that 'to refrain from writing operas required a heroism he did not possess'. *Eugene Onegin* explores real human emotions and predicaments in a Russian setting. The music is lyrical and emotional, with one highlight being the 'letter scene'. The first production was by students in Moscow, followed two years later by a professional production at the Bolshoi Theatre, Moscow.

1883   *Lakmé* by Clement Philibert [Leo] Delibes (1836–91)

A delightful body of work flowed from Delibes' pen. The classical ballets *Sylvia* and *Coppelia* show a deftness of approach, together with an appreciation of melody and all things graceful. Of the three operas he wrote for the Opera-Comique in Paris, *Lakmé* is his masterpiece.

1884   *Manon* by Jules Emile Frederic Massenet (1842–1912)

This opera marked Massenet's arrival at the winning post as most popular French opera composer of his day. Three far less successful operas followed, but *Manon*, together with his opera *Werther*, still enjoy inclusion in the modern operatic repertoire. Sadly for Massenet, his popularity waned during his lifetime, when other works such as Debussy's opera *Pelléas et Mélisande* made Massenet's work seem old fashioned.

1890   *Cavalleria Rusticana* by Pietro Mascagni (1863–1945)

This opera represents the emerging Italian fashion of *verismo*, or realist, style of opera. Although Mascagni wrote other operas, the one-act *Cavalleria Rusticana* is his only enduring work. Yet, what a work! One of the most popular musical entertainments ever, this brief masterpiece is usually twinned with Leoncavallo's equally entertaining opera, *I Pagliacci*.

1890   *Prince Igor* by Alexander Borodin (1833–87)

A doctor by profession, Borodin was to become one of the great Five Russian composers (see p. 107). He left this opera unfinished and it was completed by his friends Rimsky-Korsakov and Glazunof. Some might say Borodin had the perfect end to his life – for he dropped dead at a party.

1892   *I Pagliacci* by Ruggiero Leoncavallo (1858–1919)
In a similar way to Mascagni, Leoncavallo is thought of as a 'one opera man'. *I Pagliacci* is an enduring favourite and yet another representation of opera verismo, or 'as true to life as opera gets' (see also *La Bohème*). Although there were other operas by this composer, they have not survived into the modern repertoire, and suffered in their day from unfavourable comparison with those of Puccini.

1893   *Hansel and Gretel* by Engelbert Humperdinck (1854–1921)
Conducted by Richard Strauss at its premiere in Weimar and based on a fairytale, the opera *Hansel and Gretel* has instant appeal, both musically and dramatically. It must be considered one of *the* most appealing operas for children.

1893   *Manon Lescaut* by Giacomo Puccini (1858–1924)
The fifth generation of a family of professional musicians, Puccini, together with Verdi, is likely to spring to mind whenever Italian opera is mentioned. The composer of such enduring hits as *La Bohème*, *Tosca*, *Madame Butterfly*, *Turandot*, etc. Puccini might have been expected to enjoy universal acclaim, yet he too had his fair share of carping critics, who deplored his 'decadent' subject matter. The public loved him, however, and Bernard Shaw referred to Puccini as Verdi's successor. *Manon Lescaut*, a romantic tragedy, premiered in Turin to wild enthusiasm.

1894   *Guntram* by Richard Strauss (1864–1949)
This work, although not especially significant in its own right, marks the emergence of the great German musician Richard Strauss (not to be confused with the Viennese Strauss family) as a composer of operas. His gifted orchestral writing and insistence on using the most literary texts as bases for his libretti began to hint at a move away from the nineteenth-century predominance of Italian composers in the field of opera.

1896   *Andrea Chénier* by Umberto Giodarno (1867–1948)
An enduring success following its acclaimed premiere at La Scala, Milan, *Andrea Chénier* is a lyrical, vocally demanding opera. Set in the time of the French Revolution, it provides a good showcase for tenors. Apart from the lesser triumph of one of his other operas, *Fedora* (1898), Giodarno's compositions never again attained the level of *Andrea Chénier*.

The twentieth century

As in so many other fields, a time of development and change, with opera's popularity growing in direct response to constantly improving global communication.

1900 *Louise* by Gustave Charpentier (1860–1956)
A student of Massenet, Charpentier was both composer and librettist of this, his one successful lyrical opera. Controversial, with his blunt views on the topic of women's liberation, Charpentier carried his ideas one stage further by founding the Conservatoire Populaire Mimi Pinson, which gave free tuition in music and dancing to girls who could not otherwise have afforded such lessons.

1901 *Russalka* by Antonin Dvorak (1841–1904)
Born in Prague, son of the village butcher and publican, Dvorak was a relative latecomer to the life of a professional musician. He was nevertheless extremely successful. Sometimes known as *The Water Nymph*, *Russalka* is the most popular of his ten operas and makes an invaluable contribution to Czech operatic repertoire.

1902 *Adriana Lecouvreur* by Francesco Cilea (1866–1950)
Trained at, and in later life to become head of, the Naples Conservatoire of Music, Cilea is another composer who knew lasting operatic success with just one work. Another of his operas, *L'Arlesiana*, enjoyed modest success, prompting the publisher Sonzogno to commission *Adriana*. The latter is a wonderful vehicle for an established soprano with strong acting ability, and is full of wonderful tunes. On its opening night in Milan, the reception was rapturous, with Enrico Caruso taking the leading tenor role, Maurizio, Count of Saxony.

1902 *Pelléas and Mélisande* by Claude Achille Debussy (1862–1918)
Debussy was considered to be the founder of the Impressionist school in music. His only opera demonstrates by its free form the same criteria of suggesting an emotion, rather than stating it, that French poets of the time such as Mallarmé, Verlaine and Baudelaire strove to achieve. You will find no 'set pieces' in this opera. In his own writings, Debussy stresses that his aim is one of naturalness and spontaneity. He also adds that 'a character cannot always express himself melodically', thus answering the criticism that his opera was like one long recitative, or sung speech.

1924   *Hugh the Drover* by Ralph Vaughan Williams (1872–1958)
This English composer studied at the Royal College of Music, at Cambridge and in Berlin and Paris. Of his six operas, the first, *The Shepherds of the Delectable Mountains*, was produced in 1922 and his last, *The Pilgrim's Progress*, in 1951. A quintessentially English composer, Vaughan Williams' large body of varied work owes much to the folksong tradition.

1925   *Wozzeck* by Alban Berg (1885–1935)
This Austrian composer studied with Schoenberg to whom he dedicated another opera, *Lulu*. *Wozzeck*, premiered in Berlin in 1925, is a tragic love story with a military flavour, based on Buchner's affecting play, *Woyzeck*. Berg had experience of the army and could identify with the plight of the opera's main character. Using terse musical forms to express the play's series of short, tensely packed scenes, Berg interested himself in all aspects of the production in order to create a total artistic experience. His other opera, *Lulu*, is a more traditional work in the sense of form, and has enjoyed the same lasting popularity.

In the 20 years between the premieres of *Peter Grimes* and *Wozzeck*, more than 50 operas of varying significance and popularity were composed.

1926   *Der Protagonist* by Kurt Weill (1900–50)
Born in Germany, Kurt Weill was forced to leave in 1933. He spent some time in both Paris and London and by 1935, he was living in the United States. An interesting composer with two distinct styles allied to two very different stages in his life, Weill is certainly worthy of further study. In Germany, he composed operas in collaboration with the librettist Georg Kaiser and with Bertolt Brecht. His early works were avant-garde and frequently carried a strong political message. In his American period, Weill successfully composed musical comedies, light operas and a number of popular songs.

1945   *Peter Grimes* by Benjamin Britten (1913–76)
A prolific and important British composer, Britten wrote several significant operas. Their popularity has remained constant, and his work for children, especially *Let's make an Opera*, with its second part *The Little Sweep*, together with *The Young Person's Guide to the Orchestra* are excellent, both

for their educational and sheer entertainment value. Britten's operas show his gift for characterisation and his brilliant representation of drama. He derived inspiration from a wide range of sources and *Peter Grimes*, in particular, was felt to represent the coming-of-age of English opera. Some of his operas were premiered in Aldeburgh, at the Festival which he founded together with his friend, the English tenor, Peter Pears.

1951   *Amahl and the Night Visitors* by Gian Carlo Menotti (b. 1911)
This was the first opera written specifically for television and contains one act. It tells the story of a meeting between the Magi and a crippled boy, during the journey to Bethlehem. Menotti, an American though Italian by birth, wrote many operas, including two composed whilst he was still a child. Menotti founded the Festival of Two Worlds in Spoleto, and has made Scotland his home.

1954   *Tender Land* by Aaron Copland (1900–90)
Copland devoted himself to promoting American music, and though there was one earlier opera, *The Second Hurricane*, meant for performance in high schools, it was with this opera *Tender Land* that Copland sought to create an American opera tradition. This story of a farming community incorporates folk music and was premiered in New York.

1955   *Troilus and Cressida* by Sir William Walton (1902–83)
This English composer's love of Italian opera and all things Italian, prompted him not only to compose this opera, which premiered at Covent Garden, in the Romantic vein, but to make his home on the beautiful island of Ischia. Although a prolific and greatly valued composer, Walton wrote only one other opera, a brief one-act piece involving three characters, *The Bear*. This work was presented at the Aldeburgh Festival in 1965.

1955   *The Midsummer Marriage* by Michael Tippett (b. 1905)
Tippett wrote his own libretti, and is considered a prime moving force in the development of twentieth-century opera. His works are generally traditional in form, whilst often confronting modern-day issues. He makes use of dance and theatrical effects, while his orchestra can include saxophones and electric guitars, and he would not shrink from incorporating jazz or pop idioms.

1957   *West Side Story* by Leonard Bernstein (1918–90)
       A significant work which, together with Gershwin's *Porgy and Bess*, probably did more than any other to straddle the divide between the American musical style and classical opera. Bernstein's other works, such as the one-act *Trouble in Tahiti* and its sequel *A Quiet Place*, won critical acclaim but never achieved the success or the musically historical significance of *West Side Story*. His comic operetta *Candide* disappointed at its Broadway premiere in 1956, and this despite a strong cast and excellent production by Tyrone Guthrie. Having first achieved fame as a conductor, Bernstein continued to be in demand all his life and was a prolific composer, both for the theatre and the concert hall.

1968   *Punch and Judy* by Harrison Birtwhistle (b. 1934)
       A controversial British composer, Birtwhistle continues to challenge accepted principles and is perhaps better 'experienced', than simply listened to. A 'theatrical' composer, his work includes music for schools and even his purely instrumental work may involve a degree of movement for the musicians. His opera *Gawain*, produced at Covent Garden in 1991 and based on the fourteenth-century myth *Sir Gawain and the Green Knight*, is just as controversial as the rest, but by overstepping the bounds of what is expected, discussion is provoked, allowing opera to be catapulted into the next millennium.

MORE OPERAS BY . . .

The following list is selective, omitting details of those operas which failed to register with the public. Missing operas are numbered, allowing the scale of a composer's output to be shown.

Claudio Monteverdi

1607	*La favola d'Orfeo*
1608	*Arianna*
1618–20	*Andromeda*
1627	*La finta pazza*
1628	*Gli amore di Dafne e di Endimione*
1630	*Prosperpina rapita*
1640	*Il ritorno d'Ulisse in patria*
1641	*Le nozze d'Enea con Lavinia*
1643	*L'incoronazione di Poppea*

Henry Purcell

1689	*Dido and Aeneas*
1690	*The Prophetess* or *The History of Dioclesian*
1691	*King Arthur* or *The British Worthy*
1692	*The Fairy Queen*
1695	*The Indian Queen*

With the exception of *Dido and Aeneas*, the above works are not strictly operas, but consist of music provided for stage dramas. In *King Arthur*, the use of operatic style is so extensive and continuous it has been dubbed a 'semi-opera'.

Wolfgang Amadeus Mozart

1767	*Apollo et Hyacinthus*

1768   *Bastien und Bastienne*

At least another eight operas were written between 1768 and 1781.

1781   *Idomeneo re di Creta*
1782   *Die Entführung aus dem Serail*

Three known operas between 1782 and 1786.

1786   *Le Nozze di Figaro*
1787   *Don Giovanni*
            (full title: *Il dissoluto punito, ossia Il Don Giovanni . . . –
            The degenerate punished, or Don Giovanni*)
1790   *Così fan tutte*
            (full title: *Così fan tutte, ossi La Scuola degli amanti –
            Women are like that, or The School for Lovers*)
1791   *Die Zauberflöte* (*The Magic Flute*)
1791   *La Clemenza di Tito*

Gioacchino Antonio Rossini

As many as nine known operas preceded . . .

1813   *Tancredi*
1813   *L'italiana in Algeri*

Another three before . . .

1815   *Elisabetta, regina d'Inghilterra*

One before . . .

1816   *Le barbier de Seville*
            (originally entitled: *Almaviva, ossia L'inutile precauzione*)

Another one before . . .

1816   *Otello*
1817   *La Cenerentola*
1817   *La Gazza Ladra* (*The Thieving Magpie*)
1817   *Armida*

One before . . .

1818   *Mose in Egitto* (*Moses in Egypt*)

Two before . . .

1819   *Ermione*

Six before . . .

1823   *Semiramide*

Four before . . .

1829   *Guillaume Tell*

Gaetano Donizetti

As many as 30 operas preceded . . .

1830   *Anna Bolena*

Five before . . .

1832   *L'élisir d'amore*

Four before . . .

1833   *Lucrezia Borgia*
1833   *Maria Stuarda*

Two, plus a revision of one more before . . .

1835   *Lucia di Lammermoor*

Five before . . .

1837   *Robert Devereux*

Two, plus a second version of another before . . .

1843   *La fille du régiment* (*The daughter of the regiment*)

Seven before . . .

1843   *Don Pasquale*

Two more were to follow.

Vincenzo Bellini

1825   *Adelson e Salvini*
1826   *Bianca e Gernando*
1827   *Il pirata*
1829   *La straniera*
1829   *Zaira*
1830   *I Capuleti e Montecchi*

1831	*La Sonnambula*
1831	*Norma*
1833	*Beatrice di Tenda*
1835	*I Puritani*

Richard Wagner

1832–3	*Die Hochzeit*
1833–4	*Die Feen (The Fairies)*
1836	*Das Liebesverbot (The Ban on Love)*
1842	*Rienzi*
1843	*Der fliegende Hollander (The flying Dutchman)*
1845	*Tannhäuser* (1st version: Dresden, 2nd: Paris, 1861)
1850	*Lohengrin*
1865	*Tristan und Isolde*
1868	*Die Meistersinger von Nürnberg*
1869	*Der Ring des Nibelungen: Das Rheingold*
1870	*Die Walküre*
1876	*Siegfried*
	Götterdämmerung
1882	*Parsifal*

Giuseppe Verdi

Two operas preceded . . .

1842   *Nabucodonosor* (later *Nabucco*)

One before . . .

1844   *Ernani*

Four more before . . .

1847   *Macbeth* (revised version: Paris, 1865)

Another four before . . .

1849   *Louisa Miller*

One before . . .

1851	*Rigoletto*
1853	*Il trovatore*

1853   *La Traviata*
1857   *Simon Boccanegra* (revised 1881)

One before . . .

1859   *Un ballo in maschera*
1862   *La forza del destino* (revised 1869)
1867   *Don Carlos* (revised 1884)
1871   *Aida*
1887   *Otello*
1893   *Falstaff*

Gilbert and Sullivan

1871   *Thespis* (most of this work is lost)
1875   *Trial by Jury*
1877   *The Sorcerer*
1878   *HMS Pinafore*
1879   *The Pirates of Penzance*
1881   *Patience*
1882   *Iolanthe*
1884   *Princess Ida*
1885   *The Mikado*
1887   *Ruddigore*
1888   *The Yeoman of the Guard*
1889   *The Gondoliers*
1893   *Utopia Limited*
1896   *The Grand Duke*
NB *Cox and Box* (1867) was by F. C. Burnard and Sullivan

Peter Ilich Tchaikovsky

1869   *Voyevoda*
1869   *Undina*
1874   *Oprichnik*
1876   *Kuznets Vacula* (revised in 1887; renamed *Cherevichki*)
1879   *Eugene Onegin*
1881   *Orleanskaya deva* (*The Maid of Orleans*)
1884   *Mazeppa*
1887   *Charodeyka* (*The Enchantress*)
1890   *The Queen of Spades*
1892   *Yolanta*

Giacomo Puccini

1884	*Le villi*
1893	*Manon Lescaut*
1896	*La Bohème*
1900	*Tosca*
1904	*Madam Butterfly*
1910	*La fanciulla del West* (*The girl of the Golden West*)
1917	*La rondine*
1918	The Triptych comprising: *Il tabarro*
	Suor Angelica
	Gianni Schicchi
1926	*Turandot*
	(unfinished at the composer's death, the final scene of *Turandot* was completed by Franco Alfano)

Richard Strauss

1894	*Guntram*
1901	*Feuersnot*
1905	*Salome*
1909	*Electra*
1911	*Der Rosenkavalier*
1912	*Ariadne auf Naxos*

Although Strauss wrote another nine operas, his reputation as a composer of opera rests largely with *Salome*, *Electra*, *Der Rosenkavalier* and *Ariadne auf Naxos*.

Ralph Vaughan Williams

1922	*The Shepherds of the Delectable Mountains*
1924	*Hugh the Drover*
1929	*Sir John in Love*
1936	*The Poisoned Kiss*
1937	*Riders to the Sea*
1951	*The Pilgrim's Progress* (incorporates the one-act *The Shepherds of the Delectable Mountains*)

Benjamin Britten

1941	*Paul Bunyan*

1945	*Peter Grimes*
1946	*The Rape of Lucrezia*
1947	*Albert Herring*
1949	*Let's make an Opera; The Little Sweep*
1951	*Billy Budd*
1953	*Gloriana*
1954	*The Turn of the Screw*
1958	*Noyes Fludde*
1960	*A Midsummer Night's Dream*
1964	*Curlew River*
1966	*The Burning Fiery Furnace*
1968	*The Prodigal Son*

Strictly speaking, the last three above are religious dramas intended to be performed in church.

1971	*Owen Wingrave* (written for BBC TV)
1973	*Death in Venice*

Michael Tippett

1934	*Robin Hood*
1946–52	(produced in London, 1955) *The Midsummer Marriage*
1962	*King Priam*
1970	*The Knot Garden*
1977	*The Ice Break*
1989	*New Year*

Part Three

THE OPERA GUIDE

WOLFGANG AMADEUS MOZART (1756–91)

❛ You know my greatest desire is to write operas . . . I envy anyone
who is composing one . . . ❜
Mozart writing to his father, 4 February 1778

Joannes Chrysostomus Wolfgangus Theophilus Mozart was born on
27 January 1756, in Salzburg, a city then situated in Bavaria, now
western Austria. Leopold Mozart was in a position to recognise his
son's genius as he, too, was a brilliant musician and so was able to
give Mozart all the coaching necessary to allow him to achieve his
maximum potential. As soon as possible, a rigorous training programme was begun, and by the age of four Mozart could read music
fluently, play by ear and had begun to compose.

At six years old, under the direction of his father, Mozart visited the
courts of Europe, displaying his own skills, together with those of his
elder sister, Marianne, or 'Nannerl'. Mozart would play prepared
pieces, sight-read advanced work and improvise. He would almost
certainly have performed some of his own compositions, since he
produced minuets by the age of six, a symphony just before his ninth
birthday, his first oratorio at eleven and an opera by the age of
twelve. A virtuoso on the clavier, Mozart also played the organ and
the violin.

With his innate skills enhanced by the excellent tuition of his father,
and by his extensive travels which allowed him exposure to all manner
of European music, Mozart was able to develop and refine his genius.
It is hard to ignore the fact that his pleasure-loving and

irresponsible side may have led finally to his downfall, yet this last magical ingredient may have been the very element that allowed him to tune in so acutely to public taste.

DAINES BARRINGTON'S SCIENTIFIC STUDY

The sensation created by the nine-year-old Mozart during his visit to London in 1765 came to the attention of Daines Barrington, a Fellow of the Royal Society. His report appeared in the Society's publication, *Philosophical Transactions*.

Having first satisfied himself of the child's birth, a guarantee that proved he wasn't reviewing an adult with stunted growth, Barrington set the young child several tests. A five-part score placed before him was played on the harpsichord 'in a most masterly manner', both accurate in time and in the style intended by the composer. Next a duet, sung at sight with his father, proved straightforward for Mozart, but not so for Leopold. 'His father … was once or twice out … on which occasions the son looked back with some anger, pointing out his mistakes and setting him right.' Mozart not only sang impeccably, but also improvised a two-part accompaniment on the harpsichord whilst he sang. Next he was invited to compose on the spot two songs; one of anger and one of love. This was accomplished easily, leaving only the final test. For this he was to play a complicated piece of his own on the harpsichord. Barrington concluded 'his execution was amazing, considering that his little fingers could scarcely reach a fifth on the harpsichord.'

The Magic Flute

Background information

It seems incredible that just a little over two months after the highly successful premiere of *The Magic Flute*, Mozart would be buried in an unmarked grave.

The final period of this extraordinary life was played out at a pace, frantic even by the composer's own standards. Whilst writing *The Magic Flute* he was also composing the *Requiem* and dashing off another high-profile commission for the coronation of Leopold II, King of Bavaria, an opera seria, called *La Clemenza di Tito*. This, the seventeenth, was to be Mozart's last opera.

The mishandling of opportunities and finances, together with personal neglect, all contributed to Mozart's early death. Majoring in genius and failing in simple common sense caused him to die in poverty, a victim of his own prodigious talent.

In the eighteenth century, the rise of a successful and numerous middle class brought about the development of a new paying audience, and what they wanted was tuneful entertainment. *The Magic Flute* was the first 'popular show' written by a composer of Mozart's calibre, popular in the sense that it was not restricted to court circles, but available to anyone who could afford the entrance fee to visit, not an imperial opera house, but a small wooden theatre in Wieden (Willows), a suburb of Vienna.

Mozart had already met the actor-manager of this theatre, Emanuel Schikaneder, in Salzburg in 1773. At the time, Schikaneder had been taking the leading roles in a touring group, for which Mozart had written some incidental music.

Schikaneder was quite a showman and, unlike Mozart, understood how to turn an opportunity to his advantage. He was now in a position both to commission and to collaborate in a work in which his name would appear above that of Mozart's own. Mozart's association with Schikaneder accounts in part for the unlikely, but hugely successful, combination of comedy and profundity, stage spectacle and symbolism that is to be found in *The Magic Flute*.

Technically a Singspiel, an opera with spoken dialogue, the form was developed by Mozart so far beyond its original state that *The Magic Flute* may be considered the first of the truly great German operas.

Schikaneder wrote the libretto together with a young student, Carl Ludwig Giesecke. Carl's real name was Metzler, but he wanted to make certain that his academic colleagues were not alerted to the fact that he was working as a 'jack of all trades' at the theatre, in order to pay his way through university. With these ingredients – Mozart, the musical genius, Giesecke, the academic and Schikaneder, the show-man – the unlikely mix of style and approach in *Flute* becomes more understandable.

Mozart was both a practising Catholic and a Freemason, and there are many allusions to the masonic brotherhood and their principles in *The Magic Flute*.

Although Schikaneder was also a Freemason, it seems likely that it would have been Giesecke, the academic, who sourced much of the information on masonic symbolism from a popular book of the time, *Sethos*, written by Abbé Terrasson.

It was the custom for a composer to write parts for specific singers to perform and Schikaneder, undoubtedly quite a well-known personality, saw to it that a role of the type for which he was renowned was created. *Papageno*, the birdcatcher, is a significant, humourous part, with every opportunity to show off a good voice.

Terribly sick, and working under ferocious pressure, Mozart takes us on a journey to a mythical land full of joy, fun, spirituality, brotherly love and great tunes.

Fairytale, allegory, pantomime, spiritually intense, *The Magic Flute* is all of these, yet rather than lacking focus, the vastly different elements are effortlessly combined, producing a master work of enduring appeal.

Characters

Tamino, an Egyptian prince — **Tenor**; male romantic lead

Three ladies, Queen of the Night's attendants — **Two sopranos** and a **Mezzo-soprano**; plot movers

Papageno, a bird catcher — **Baritone**; comic relief

The Queen of the Night — **Colaratura soprano**; extremely bad female

Monostatos, a moor, the servant of Sarastro — **Tenor**; extremely bad male

Pamina, Queen of the Night's daughter — **Soprano**; female romantic lead

Three genii, servants of The Queen of the Night — Three **boy trebles** *or* two **sopranos** and one **mezzo-soprano**; surprisingly good considering their employer's reputation

Sarastro, high priest of Isis and Osiris	**Bass**; Moses-like figure of unimpeachable reputation
Three priests	**Tenor** and **two bass**; someone has to keep discipline
Papagena	**Soprano**; female comic relief
Two men in armour	**Tenor** and **bass**; more disciplinarians

Many singers have excelled in the exceptionally demanding role of Queen of the Night, but few have brought the enthusiasm and rather unique approach of Florence Foster Jenkins. If you can possibly obtain a recording of this astonishing lady, who on 25 October 1944, at the age of 76, filled the Carnegie Hall, you must do so. High coloratura was Florence Foster Jenkin's 'speciality', especially after a crash in a taxi-cab in 1943, when she found she could sing a higher note than ever before. The taxi driver was rewarded with a large box of expensive cigars.

Plot structure and summary

Structure

The Magic Flute, Mozart's sixteenth opera, defies categorisation since it successfully combines a number of elements, such as comedy, myth and ritual. There are two acts and, depending upon a particular interpretation, as many as 13 scenes; three scenes in Act One and ten in Act Two. Judging by the number of scenes, you might expect there to be plenty going on. You would be right!

The running time is approximately 2 hours and 40 minutes.

Summary

In a mythological land, Tamino is running away from a giant serpent. Three ladies kill the beast as our hero faints. Papageno arrives and introduces himself, but the ladies are not impressed and padlock his mouth. When Tamino wakes, the ladies show him a miniature portrait of Pamina, daughter of The Queen of the Night. Tamino falls in love at once.

The Queen of the Night appears, to say that Tamino may marry her daughter when he has rescued Pamina from Sarastro, high priest of Isis and Osiris. The three ladies give Tamino a magic flute to help him in his quest and then free Papageno, who is to accompany Tamino. The moor, Monastatos, plans to rape Pamina, but luckily Papageno arrives in time to prevent this.

Meanwhile, three boys lead Tamino to the temple, where he embarks upon a course of self-improvement. Papageno arrives with Pamina. The two young lovers are ecstatic, but before they may marry, Tamino must undergo a number of trials.

Papageno, who has been quite jolly so far and all for no tangible reward, is finally allowed a glimpse of a Papagena, who will be his if he behaves himself to the end of the opera.

The Queen of the Night wants Sarastro dead so that she can rule during the day as well as at night. She hands her daughter a knife, but Pamina is not the murdering kind. Visiting Tamino during the period of his trials, she does not realise that he has promised to be silent. Fearing he no longer loves her, Pamina thinks of taking her own life with the knife.

The three boys arrive in time to save Pamina and take her to Tamino. The young lovers endure the final trials together and emerge triumphant.

Papageno is reunited with Papagena. The Queen of the Night and Monastatos plot to kill Sarastro and his followers, but they are foiled by the rays of the rising sun.

All the virtuous characters are now able to praise Isis and Osiris for delivering them from the evil clutches of the Queen of the Night and her cronies.

Comment

Don't expect every opera plot to be zany as *The Magic Flute*'s. Characters such as Papageno, the birdcatcher, may have had some humorous connotation in their day, but that relevance is largely lost to us now. You might imagine an audience of the time nudging each other delightedly as a well-known player shuffled on-stage in Papageno's fantastic feathered costume, and commenting 'What's the old devil up to now?' The original cast were, after all, playing to their loyal fans.

There is a theory that Monostatos represented a repressive view of the Catholic Church, another theory has him representing a man called Hoffmann, a maverick freemason who denounced the lodges to the government as subversive. Did Pamina represent the Austrian people; The Queen of the Night, Empress Maria Theresa; Tamino, Joseph II, Maria Theresa's son? Or were the rumours started to add the spice of scandal to the opera's publicity? Whatever the truth might be, don't worry about trying to make sense of the storyline, because no one ever has completely! The fact that it is all a glorious jumble shouldn't detract from your enjoyment of an entertainment as appealing today as it was on 30 September 1791.

Listen out for

There is some recitative and lots of talking in this opera, but the action moves along at a hectic pace, and the variety and quality of the music ensures that you will never be bored.

As there are so many scenes in this opera, it is simpler to ignore subdivisions and divide it into acts.

Act One

Immediately	*Orchestra*	*Overture* A solemn start gives way to a rush of music that forms a mouthwatering introductory tune. Listen out for the famous three chords that are supposedly representative of the three knocks used in masonic ceremonies. The agitated music at curtain-up reveals Tamino's plight.
15 mins	*Papageno*	*Der Vogelfänger bin ich ja* A most entertaining introduction to this character.
20 mins	*Tamino*	*Dies Bildnis ist bezaubernd schön* Glorious expression of love at first sight.
30 mins	*Queen of the Night*	*O zitt're nicht, mein lieber Sohn!* Angry woman tries to stay calm.

| 50 mins | Papageno/
Pamina | *Bei Männern welche Liebe fühlen*
Lovely duet exalting the state of love. |

Act Two

5 mins	Sarastro	*O Isis und Osiris* Stunning bass aria to whistle on the way home.
20 mins	Queen of the Night	*Der Hölle Rache* 'The revenge of hell boils in my heart'; angry woman makes no attempt to stay calm.
25 mins	Sarastro	*In diesen heil'gen Hallen* 'Within these holy bounds'; sonorous bass aria representing the forces of good.
35 mins	Pamina	*Ach, ich fühl's* Wistful love song of great beauty.
70 mins	Pamina	*Tamino mein* Lovers reunited; change of key and pace add consequence to this magical moment.
80 mins	Papageno/ Papagena	*Pa pa pa, etc* Truly ridiculous duet, perfectly suited to these two.
90 mins	Chorus	*Heil sei euch Geweihten* 'Hail ye souls enlightened'; provides a worthy climax to this most entertaining opera.

Postscript

Almost immediately, *The Magic Flute* was a great success; at first amongst German-speaking people and then right across Europe.

Many people tried to claim responsibility for the libretto and format of the show – for show it was, in the sense of whizz-bang, non-stop entertainment.

In fairness, it seems likely that Schikaneder's experienced troupe of players and backstage helpers would have contributed ideas as the rehearsals got underway. Mozart lived close by at the time and would have been able to respond quickly to any suggestions or changes. Sustaining popularity and innovation for a regular audience meant theatrical effects must have figured almost as high on the list of requirements as the music itself. Mozart's music enhances and supports these affects, whilst transcending mere theatrical jiggery-pokery.

Creating a new, previously undreamed-of standard for popular entertainment, whilst simultaneously pushing forward the boundaries of classical composition, is one of the most striking measures of this composer's genius.

Mozart writes from Vienna to his wife, Constanze, 7 October 1791

'During Papageno's aria with the glockenspiel I went behind the scenes, as I felt a sort of impulse today to play it myself. Well, just for fun, at the point where Schikaneder has a pause, I played an arpeggio. He was startled, looked behind the wings and saw me. When he had his next pause, I played no arpeggio. This time he stopped and refused to go on. I guessed what he was thinking and again played a chord. He then struck the glockenspiel and said, "*shut up*"! Whereupon everybody laughed. I am inclined to think that this joke taught many of the audience for the first time that Papageno does not play the instrument himself.'

Recommended recordings

With Kiri Te Kanawa as Pamina and Sir Neville Marriner, founder of the Academy of St Martin in the Fields, conducting, plus a sensational Queen of the Night by the American soprano Cheryl Studer, the Philips digital recording is superb.

If you have enjoyed this, now try . . .

Mozart's opera *The Marriage of Figaro* is mentioned several times during the course of this book and is every bit as entertaining as *The Magic Flute*. It is such a popular inclusion in the repertoire of most opera companies that it should be fairly easy for you to visit a live performance.

GIOACCHINO ANTONIO ROSSINI
(1792–1868)

❦ There is nothing to composing, it's rehearsals that are tiresome. That's the miserable moment when the poor maestro endures real torture hearing his finest inspirations distorted in every tone of which the human voice is capable. ❦
  Stendhal, *Life of Rossini*, translation by Stephen Brook

The most influential Italian opera composer of the first part of the nineteenth century, Rossini built upon the opera seria and opera buffa traditions of the previous century. His genius for melody, wit, catchy rhythms and thrilling musical showmanship, enabled him to transform these earlier forms, and in particular opera buffa, into a profusion of enduringly popular music.

Born in Pesaro to musical parents, Rossini by the age of 14 had mastered the harpsichord, horn, violin, cello and he also sang professionally. Keen to pursue his studies in composition, in 1806 he entered the Bologna conservatory, where he wrote his first opera, *Demetrio e Polibio*.

In 12 years, between the ages of 18 and 30, Rossini produced 32 operas and two oratorios. In 1813, aged only 21, his opera *Tancredi* was staged at the Teatro la Fenice in Venice. One of his greatest works, *Tancredi* is not in the light-hearted style most usually associated with this composer, but there were more serious operas to come, including *Otello* (1816), *Mose in Egitto* (1818), *Maometto II* (1820), and *Semiramide* (1823).

In the same year as *Otello*, Rossini's masterpiece *Il Barbiere di Siviglia*, originally known as *Almaviva, ossia L'inutile precauzione*, was staged in Rome. This astonishing workrate was the norm rather than the exception for Rossini, who thought nothing of dashing off an opera and for whom rehearsals seemed to provide the only temporary brake to his creativity. On hearing that Rossini had written *The Barber* in two weeks, Donizetti remarked, tongue in cheek, 'It does not surprise me, he was always lazy.'

One of Rossini's many strengths was that he organised his operas so that the audience knew what to expect. A splendid, attention-grabbing overture, sensational arias for the soloist, memorable tunes, musical showmanship throughout and sensible divisions of the work into acts proved a winning formula.

In Italy especially, Rossini-mania surpassed anything known before, or since. A letter written by Leigh Hunt in 1823 to the English organist and music publisher Vincent Novello asserts 'Mozart is nothing in Italy and Rossini, everything!'

Reports talk of melodies by Rossini being 'demi-semi-quavered from morning to night', and apart from the truth of this as far as the popularity of his music was concerned, Rossini didn't believe in using one note where a dozen might do!

In about 1835 Rossini became director of the Theatre-Italien in Paris and settled in this city with his wife. Apparently completely unspoiled by his celebrity, when invited to compose a number of stage works for this theatre by the French government, he first engaged in a period of thorough familiarisation with both French literature and the French mode of expression. He also chose the singers himself and then trained them in the *bel canto* tradition.

This thoughtful approach brought him even more resounding success, culminating in his Grand Opera *Guillaume Tell*, which was staged in Paris in 1829. Unlike many of his other works, this opera was not dashed off, but worked on diligently over a period of time. With a now-famous overture and some undeniable high spots, despite its length (four acts in almost four hours), *Guillaume Tell* was the closest Rossini came to composing in the Romantic opera style.

Guillaume Tell was Rossini's last work for the stage, and it's hard to tell whether his lack of interest in the increasingly fashionable Romantic style caused his withdrawal from such a high-profile professional life. What *is* known, is that at the age of 39, apart from two religious works, a number of songs and some albums for the piano, this immeasurably popular composer simply retired from public life.

The Barber of Seville

Background information

Possibly the most frequently performed of any opera and reputedly composed in two frenzied weeks, *The Barber of Seville* reflects its composer's temperament: fresh, full of fizz and bursting with good tunes.

Sterbini's libretto was based on Beaumarchais' original comedy, *Le Barbier de Seville*. This was already interspersed with song and by following this well-laid-out plan, Sterdini was able to create one of the finest libretti ever set by Rossini.

The overture, one of the composer's best, had been used before in at least two previous operas: *Aureliano in Palmira* (Milan, 1813) and *Elisabetta, regina d'Inghilterra* (Naples, 1815). This 'cherry-picking' of parts of a previous work was certainly not restricted to Rossini, and may go part of the way to explaining why some composers managed to turn out such a vast quantity of work in what seems now to have been an impossibly short space of time.

After this huge build-up, you may be disappointed to learn that the first performance in Rome in 1816 of the original version, then called *Almaviva, ossia L'inutile precauzione*, (so named to differentiate Rossini's *Barber* from an earlier version (1782) by the composer, Giovanni Paisiello) was a complete and utter disaster. Rossini might just as well have suppressed his finer feelings towards the older composer, for Paisiello's supporters turned out in force to heckle the opening night of Rossini's opera. First-night hitches compounded the disaster as Don Basilio fell through an open trap door and a stray cat wandered across the stage.

The second night was more successful, but a short season at the Teatro Argentina prevented the work from becoming properly established.

The title, *Il Barbieri di Siviglia*, was first used in Bologna later in 1816, and it would be five years more before *The Barber* played again in Rome.

After this less-than-propitious start, it is not surprising that a breathing space required before the work could be given a fair hearing. It didn't help that critics in England, France and Germany were largely dismissive and compared the work unfavourably with that of Paisiello. Fortunately for posterity, the public was the final judge and Rossini's *Barber* overcame every handicap, to establish itself as one of the most popular operas of all time.

Characters

Fiorello, the Count's servant	**Bass**; obviously run off his feet by the Count, since he only has time to make a brief appearance.
Count Almaviva, also known as *Lindoro*	**Tenor**; the wit of this man does little for the reputation of the aristocracy. If only he would spend less time masquerading and more time asserting himself . . . . Nevertheless, male romantic lead.
Figaro, a barber	**Baritone**; Mr Fix-it and he hasn't aged a day since his marriage was celebrated by Mozart 30 years before.
Doctor Bartolo, elderly and unattractive	**Bass**; The girl has to be won from someone – this is the man.
Rosina, clever little minx and ward of Doctor Bartolo	**Soprano**; (sung by a mezzo, a richer voice-type Rossini loved, in the earliest productions). Female romantic lead.
Don Basilio, a singing teacher	**Bass**; presumably extremely unattractive since he is allowed access to Rosina.
Berta, Rosina's governess	**Soprano**; Aged crone who has a hard time of it putting up with Bartolo, attempts to decipher the convoluted plot and has some of the best lines about love.

Ambrogio, Doctor Bartolo's servant	**Bass**; a man of the Doctor's standing should have a servant, and this is he.

One of the most popular baritones to play the part of Figaro in *The Barber of Seville* was a Puerta Rican named Pablo Elvira. Considered to be one of the two best trumpet players in Puerto Rico, Elvira had already made a great success out of performing with his own dance band, when he was inspired to try singing by the film *The Great Caruso*, starring Mario Lanza.

Years of dedicated study paid off, resulting in a technique of enviable beauty and ease.

Elvira appeared at the New York City Opera for several seasons, and played both Tonio in *I Pagliacci*, and Figaro in *The Barber of Seville* at the Metropolitan Opera House, New York.

Plot summary and structure

Structure

The *Barber of Seville* is an opera buffa in two acts, with two scenes in each act. Act One is by far the longer, with an approximate running time of 90 minutes; Act Two is about half that length.

Think of any silent movie comedy and you've got the storyline about right.

Summary

The curtain opens on a courtyard at dawn, in seventeenth-century Spain, outside Rosina's bedroom window. Count Almaviva, masquerading as Lindoro, is serenading Rosina. She is a heavy sleeper, however, so the Count gives up and dismisses his musicians. Figaro arrives, introduces himself, and assures the Count that he will be able to get him into the house. Not only is he employed by the owner, Doctor Bartolo, but he is able to reassure the Count on another point; Rosina is merely the doctor's ward and not his daughter.

Figaro persuades the Count to try again, and this time Rosina appears on her balcony. After a moment, she disappears with a shriek. Figaro comes up with a scheme to get the Count into the house. He is to dress as a drunken soldier and demand a billet for the night. Cheered by this ludicrous proposition, the Count asks for directions to Figaro's shop, so that he may reward him.

Meanwhile, Rosina makes plans to smuggle out a letter to the mysterious Lindoro. Her singing teacher, Don Basilio arrives and warns Doctor Bartolo that the lecherous Count Almaviva is sniffing around Rosina. Doctor Bartolo is extremely jealous and determines to marry the girl himself.

Figaro overhears everything and smuggles out Rosina's letter. The Count arrives in his guise of a drunken soldier. Doctor Bartolo is not impressed and calls the guard. The Count alerts the guard to his true identity and determines to try again.

Returning this time in the guise of Don Basilio, the Count finds himself alone with Rosina. Imagining him to be the mysterious Lindoro, Rosina declares her love. Unfortunately, the real Don Basilio turns up, expecting to give Rosina her singing lesson. The Count pays him off.

The Count and Figaro return that evening to steal Rosina. She is confused and imagines that her minstrel lover, Lindoro, means to sacrifice her to the lusts of the dreaded Count Almaviva. Lindoro reveals his true identity and all is bliss, or at least until they discover that the ladder placed by the window to allow them to escape has disappeared.

Don Basilio arrives with the Notary, who imagines he is to perform a wedding ceremony for Doctor Bartolo and Rosina. Figaro sets them straight, whilst the Count employs his infallible bribery tactics once again. Doctor Bartolo must resign himself to the inevitable and Rosina and Count Almaviva live happily ever after . . . or at least until you meet them again in *The Marriage of Figaro*.

Listen out for . . .

Act One; Scene One

Immediately   *Orchestra*   *Overture*

This is strictly a 'grab their attention and leave them in no doubt they're in for a rich helping of Rossini at his best and cover the sound of shuffling as they find their seat' type of Overture. In other words, there is no reference whatever to the melodies to come, although the mood of comic chaos is firmly established. The opening blast alerts everyone to the fact that they had better settle down and then, after a moment or two's waffling, the orchestra settles into a briskly memorable and technically impressive piece. Notes tumble hectically over each other and the pace may, or may not, depending upon the skills of the orchestra, increase. Crescendos build and subside with increasing regularity, bringing the listener to a positive fever-pitch of excitement. A grand finale tells you exactly when to applaud . . . How can you resist?

10 mins	*Count Almaviva*	*Ecco ridente in cielo* Pretty song; Count plays the innocent.
20 mins	*Figaro*	*Largo al factotum* 'Top of the pops' as Figaro introduces himself.
30 mins	*Count Almaviva*	*Se il mio nome saper voi bramante* Very pretty song, but we know what he's after.

Act One; Scene Two

Immediately	*Rosina*	*Un voce poco fa* Excitable young lady dreams of a lover.
10 mins	*Don Basilio*	*La calunnia* Plotter plans to discredit the Count.
20 mins	*Rosina/Figaro*	*Dunque io son* Dreaming of pleasures to come.
26 mins	*Bartolo*	*A un dotter della mia sorte* The good doctor fears that he has been duped and sings an angry though melodious ditty.

| 31 mins | *Tutti* | *Finale*
Everyone yells at each other;
translated for operatic purposes
into ensemble singing both sublime
and exciting. |

Act Two; Scene One

| 7 mins | *Rosina / Count* | *Contro un cor*
Passion confessed. |
| 21 mins | *Rosina / Count /*
Figaro / Bartolo /
Basilio | *Buona sera mio signore*
Almost everyone gets a chance to
have their say. The pace quickens;
more notes, more crescendo, more
everything. |

Act Two; Scene Two

| 10 mins | *Rosina / Count /*
Figaro | *Ah, qual colpo inaspettato*
A joyous trio as Lindoro reveals his
true identity. |
| 18 mins | *Tutti* | *Finale*
Joy! Rapture! . . . and everyone
shall live happily ever after – until
The Marriage of Figaro. |

A CAUTIONARY TALE

It's easy to become confused between Mozart's *Marriage of Figaro* and Rossini's *Barber of Seville*, because both libretti have been based upon characters that appear in Beaumarchais' trilogy of plays. Even more confusing is the fact that the *Barber* story is the first play in the trilogy, since Rosina is being wooed by the Count, whereas in *The Marriage of Figaro*, set by Mozart 30 years earlier, she is his Countess. In *Marriage*, Bartolo – who is Rosina's guardian in *Barber* – turns out to be Figaro's father, yet in *Barber*, Bartolo is a lecherous old bachelor who doesn't appear to know his son and seems an unlikely choice of guardian for the young Rosina. No one said understanding opera was going to be easy, or even possible, but the music's great, so sit back and enjoy it!

Postscript

The libretti for Mozart's *Marriage of Figaro* and for Rossini's *Barber of Seville* were taken from two plays of a trilogy written by the French playwright and amateur musician, Pierre Augustin Caron de Beaumarchais (1732–99). The third play, *La mere coupable*, was set by Darius Milhaud in the twentieth century. In this last of the three plays, the Countess has a baby by the young page, Cherubino – which confuses the issue further still, since the Countess is usually taken to be at least old enough to be Cherubino's mother . . . .

Recommended recordings

No one has quite the mischief in the voice for the part of Rosina, nor of course the power to communicate, of Maria Callas. For her inimitable performance alone, it would be worth purchasing the EMI Classics recording with the Philharmonia Orchestra and Chorus conducted by Alceo Galliera. As a priceless bonus, the part of Figaro is sung by Tito Gobbi.

If you have enjoyed this, now try . . .

La Cenerentola is the story of Cinderella, with even more demanding vocal fireworks for the mezzo-soprano lead in this ever-popular tale of virtue rewarded. Coming just a year after *The Barber of Seville*, the story is droll and touching, with a lost bracelet substituting for that famous lost slipper . . . perhaps trying-on shoes whilst singing fit to bust was just a bit too much to ask of the soprano!

GIUSEPPE VERDI
(1813–1901)

An innkeeper's son from the village of La Roncole in Italy, Verdi knew real adversity, having narrowly escaped a massacre as a child, and in adult life losing to illness both his young wife and two infant children.

He received his first music lessons from the village organist, and by the time he was 12, was sufficiently advanced to merit payment when he stood in for his teacher. He failed, however, to win a scholarship to the music conservatory in Milan, because, it was said, he showed no aptitude for music.

Undeterred and aided by a grant from his native region, Verdi continued his musical studies in Milan with Vincenzo Lavigna, a composer and professional musician at La Scala. Once his studies were completed, Verdi returned home to commence work as a small-town musician. In 1836 he completed his first opera *Rocester* (now lost) and married Margherita Barezzi, his patron's daughter.

In 1839, his opera *Oberto* was accepted by La Scala, thanks partly to the support of the young leading soprano, Giuseppina Strepponi, who, in 1859, would become his second wife. After the success of *Oberto*, Verdi was commissioned to write three more operas, but the death of his young wife, following so swiftly after the death of his two children, reduced Verdi to despair. Bartolomeo Merelli, the manager of La Scala, finally tempted him back to work with Temistocle Solera's libretto, *Nabucodonosor*. Later known as *Nabucco*, this was to be the first of many outstanding works.

Verdi's 26 operas were written between 1839 and 1893, making his a creative life of unusual longevity, and, apart from the *Requiem*, a string quartet, some settings of sacred works and a number of songs, all of Verdi's professional life centred on the stage. From 1839 to 1867 Verdi established his position, and from 1867 onwards he was able to enjoy the fruits of his success. Retiring to his country retreat, Verdi knew the luxury of writing for pleasure and relaxation, which provoked greater interest than ever from both public and music critics alike. Verdi abhorred publicity, and so when his opera *Otello* was staged in Milan in 1887, the city was bursting at the seams with excited visitors and locals, all curious to know what new marvel could possibly issue from the pen of their musical hero who was now a 73 year-old 'gentleman farmer'. Confident that he wouldn't disappoint them, during the final rehearsals crowds gathered to cheer the old man as he arrived, or left the theatre. At curtain-down on the opening night, the audience went crazy. A huge crowd had gathered outside, and as Verdi stepped into his carriage, it was his fellow countrymen, rather than horses, who drew the carriage to his home!

Verdi's appeal lies in his ability to utilise a wider musical palette than ever before, which enabled him to paint life with his music in a particularly vivid and affecting way. Knowing something of his history, it is perhaps not surprising that, unlike Richard Wagner who was born in the same year, Verdi had no time for myths and mystery, but preferred to confront real human issues and emotions. He was not an innovator, but a refiner of an art that blossomed as never before under the influence of his creative impetus.

A dignified and modest figure who was very much the patriot, Verdi's works clearly reflected his deeply felt ideals. His music spoke of national unity and the avoidance of foreign influences, endearing him all the more to Italian patriots, to whom even his name was a rallying cry; 'Viva Verdi!' meant in effect, 'Viva Vittorio Emanuele Re d'Italia', 'Long live Victor Emanuel, King of Italy'. When he died, the nation mourned, and as his coffin passed through the streets of Milan, the huge crowd who had gathered spontaneously sang *Va, pensiero*, the poignant chorus of the Hebrew slaves from Verdi's opera *Nabucco*.

La Traviata

Background information

This opera is the culmination of the first period of Verdi's creative life. By the age of 40 he had composed 19 operas and *La Traviata*, the last of these, shows a real confidence in its use of orchestral colour to promote dramatic realism.

With a libretto written by Franceso Maria Piave and based upon the novel *La dame aux camélias*, by Dumas the younger, realism is exactly what this opera is based upon.

The beautiful young courtesan, Marie Duplessis, upon whose life the character Violetta is based, was famous throughout Paris. She died at the age of 23, only three months before Verdi visited Paris, denying him a glimpse of his heroine in the flesh. Both innovative and daring, because of the contemporary and racy nature of its subject matter, *La Traviata*, or 'the woman who has gone astray', confronts issues and emotions affecting real people and allows an audience to identify more closely with the characters than ever before.

Characters

Violetta Valery, a high-society courtesan
Soprano; female romantic lead

Flora Bervoix, a friend of Violetta
Mezzo-soprano; enjoys a less complicated life than Violetta

Marchèse d'Obigny, elderly aristocrat
Bass; Flora's friend

Annina, Violetta's maid
Soprano; faithful to the end

Le Vicomte Gaston de Letorières, young aristocrat
Tenor; A friend of Alfredo

Alfredo Germont, society figure
Tenor; male romantic lead; become Violetta's lover

Baron Douphol, Violetta's 'sugar daddy'	**Baritone**; despite being treated shabbily, the Baron loves Violetta throughout
Georgio Germont, Alfredo's father	**Baritone**; disapproving, but utterly principled
Doctor Grenvil	**Bass**; bringer of bad tidings
Giuseppe, Violetta's servant	
Commissario, messenger	

Plot structure and summary

Structure

La Traviata is an opera in three acts with two intervals. Act Two has two scenes. The running time is approximately 1 hour 50 minutes.

Summary

The young courtesan, Violetta, enjoys the protection of Baron Douphol. She is introduced to Alfredo by a mutual friend, Gaston de Letorières.

Alfredo has loved Violetta from afar for some time, even visiting her house many times to enquire after her health during a recent bout of illness. Violetta says she can offer him only friendship.

Alfredo persists and finally they set up home together. Alfredo's father Georgio visits Violetta and accuses her of living off immoral earnings supplied by his son. Violetta denies this absolutely; in fact, it is she who is supporting Alfredo. Georgio next tells her that the scandal will prevent his daughter from marrying. Hearing this, Violetta softens and despite his earlier misgivings, Georgio is much affected by her sincerity as she vows to sacrifice her relationship with his son.

Alfredo returns home to find that Violetta is attending a party at her friend Flora's house. He is incensed to hear that the Baron is her escort and hurries off to confront them both.

A wonderful party is in full swing when Alfredo arrives. Violetta warns him that the Baron will not tolerate his presence. Alfredo ignores her advice and goes to the gaming tables. He wins a great deal of money, and, returning to confront Violetta, throws the money at her feet, declaring his debt to her settled. The whole company is aghast and even Alfredo's father declares himself horrified that his son could behave so shabbily. Violetta is dying. Alfredo and his father arrive in time; one to declare his undying love and the other to express his remorse. With a blessing for any future wife of Alfredo's Violetta dies.

Listen out for . . .

There is practically no 'padding' at all in this opera; every moment of music intensifies and advances the drama.

Act One

Immediately	*Orchestra*	*Prelude*
		Exquisitely heart-wrenching music laced with elegantly happy themes sets the scene. Energetic bustle as the curtain rises on a party.
10 mins	*Alfredo / Violetta / Tutti*	*Brindisi* Jolly drinking song.
15 mins	*Alfredo / Violetta*	*Un dì felice* A most beautiful declaration of love by Alfredo, countered by Violetta's offer of friendship.
22 mins	*Violetta*	*Ah fors'e lui che l'anima* Glorious consideration of the advantages of true love versus feckless pleasure.
27 mins	*Violetta*	*Sempre libera* Leading straight on from *Ah fors'e lui*, and in spite of interjections off by Alfredo, it seems, for now, that feckless pleasure wins the day.

Act Two

Immediately	*Alfredo*	*Lunga da lei per me ... O mio rimorso*
		Alfredo holds the stage, give or take an interjection or two by Annina, for around ten stirring minutes.

| 15 mins | *Germont* | *Pura siccome un angelo*
 Alfredo's father pleads his daughter's cause – the shame of her brother's dalliance with a courtesan will ruin her plans to marry. |

As Germont begins to see Violetta's fine character and feels the pain of her sacrifice, he warms to her and the music for them both grows ever more poignant and beautiful.

| 22 mins | *Violetta* | *Dite alla giovine si bella e pura*
 Heartbreaking pledge. |
| | *Germont* | *Piangi, o misera, piangi!*
 Weep, unhappy girl, weep! I see the sacrifice I ask .... |

Every moment until the next major aria by Germont is full of glorious music – and so it continues right up to the end of the scene.

| 35 mins | *Germont* | *Mio figlio Oh, quanto soffri!*
 My son, I know how much you suffer. |

Act Two; Scene Two

| 50 minutes | *Tutti* | *Finale; Disprezzo degno se stesso rende ...*
 Germont is disgusted by Alfredo's treatment of Violetta.
 Alfredo: What have I done?
 Tutti to *Violetta*: We are all your friends.
 Baron to *Alfredo*: You shall suffer for this.
 Violetta: Know how much I love you, Alfredo .... |

Act Three

| Immediately | *Orchestra* | Light, spiritual music by the string section sets the scene for Violetta's death scene. |

Poignant moments follow between Violetta, Annima, and later, Doctor Grenvil.

12 mins	*Violetta*	*Addio, del passato* Farewell, happy dreams of days gone by.
20 mins	*Alfredo /* *Violetta*	*O mia Violetta* Rapturous reunion.
22 mins	*Alfredo /* *Violetta*	*Parigi, o cara, noi lasceremo* Distressingly hopeless plans.
35 mins	*Violetta*	*Se una pudica vergine* A blessing for the wife Alfredo may take when Violetta is dead.

Postscript

Marie Duplessis enjoyed as much celebrity in mid nineteenth-century Paris, as any latter-day beauty with all the modern benefits of media hype. Reports of the time leave a fleeting impression of youth, grace, charm, great beauty, stunning jewels and ravishing costumes.

When Marie died at the tragically early age of 23, ladies who would not have given her so much as a nod when she was alive, queued outside her home, hoping to buy anything at all that had belonged to this celebrated, yet as far as 'polite' society was concerned, outcast young woman.

Immortalised in the novel *La dame aux camélias*, written by Dumas the younger, with whom she had been reputed to have had a brief, but passionate affair, the tragic, star-burst life of Marie Duplessis also captured Verdi's imagination. No stranger himself to strong emotions, his very genius lay in translating the trials and triumphs of human existence into music and, even if the words were removed, each element of *La Traviata*'s story-line would still be just as vividly portrayed in his music.

Like many personalities who have passed into legend, Marie Duplessis could not know how many treasures her brief life would inspire. Her grave, with its wreath of camellias captured beneath a glass case, lies in the cemetery of Montmartre, where 'Alphonsine Duplessis', her childhood name, is carved on the modest square headstone.

Recommended recordings

The sublime Joan Sutherland in the role of the tragic heroine, Violetta, plus a young and stunningly vibrant Luciano Pavarotti in the role of Alfredo, takes some beating. Joan Sutherland's husband, Richard Bonynge conducts the National Philharmonic Orchestra in this digital recording from Decca.

If you have enjoyed this, now try . . .

Aida is an opera on a really grand scale, and with double helpings of everything you might expect. Riveting drama, glorious music and spectacle by the bucketful. A popular inclusion at the open-air arena in Verona, this work was first staged at the Cairo opera house in 1871. Verdi received a draft of the libretto in 1870, which must have seemed absolutely in tune with the general interest in Egypt at that time, following the opening of both the Suez Canal and the Cairo Opera House in 1869.

GEORGES BIZET
(1838–75)

Bizet was a musical child who received his first music lessons from his parents and then entered the Paris Conservatory at the age of nine. An outstanding pianist and composer, at the age of 19 he shared a prize, given by the composer Offenbach, for his setting of a one-act operetta. Later that same year he won the prestigious Prix de Rome and travelled to that city to continue his musical studies. Four works survive from this period, including an opera buffa, *Don Procopio*, although this was not performed until 1906. Bizet returned to Paris after three years and rather than developing a career as a concert pianist, or accepting a teaching post at the conservatory, he devoted himself to fulfilling one of the terms of the Prix de Rome, which was to compose an opera.

It would be fair to say that Bizet took some time to develop fully as a composer of opera, and whether due to weak libretti, or musical writing that had yet to mature fully, his earlier works were not strong enough to survive the passage of time.

Apart from his outstanding opera *Carmen*, only *The Pearl Fishers*, *The Fair Maid of Perth* and *Djamileh* have survived as occasional inclusions in modern repertoire.

Carmen is head and shoulders above these other compositions, both as the first real example of opera verismo, with its uncompromisingly gritty plotline, and because of Bizet's sensitive handling of musical themes to create associations with characters, events and emotions.

Bizet was never to know the incredible triumph that Carmen would enjoy and certainly could not have appreciated its importance as a landmark in the development of opera. He died at the age of only 37, just three months after the first performance, at which time the opera was booed off stage.

Carmen

Background information

France, and, in particular, Paris society was undergoing a reappraisal of moral values following the perceived excesses of the Second Empire. The Opéra Comique theatre itself was a morally irreproachable house, where families could be guaranteed an evening of respectable entertainment. *Carmen* must have scandalised the staid audience, with a fallen woman for its heroine and one, furthermore, who showed neither remorse, nor displayed the slightest intention of reforming her character. In a general mood of disapprobation, the singers declared the music unsingable, and the musicians, the music unplayable. The opera staggered on for 45 performances, panned by critics and public alike.

Fortunately, a production in Vienna later that same year was received with the enthusiasm that *Carmen* has enjoyed ever since. Composers such as Wagner, Richard Strauss and Tchaikovsky expressed their admiration for this exceptional work, with its innovative use of orchestra and singers vividly recreating the passionate ambience of Mediterranean life and temperament. The only cautious and sometimes sour note would come from Spain, for Bizet was thoroughly French, yet had managed to encapsulate what people worldwide now believed to be the music of Spain.

Characters

Carmen, a gypsy girl working in a cigarette factory — **Mezzo-soprano**; sexually provocative female lead

Don José, a corporal — **Tenor**; male romantic lead

Escamillo, a bullfighter — **Baritone**; popular local hero

Micaëla, country girl	**Soprano**; purity personified
Zuniga, a lieutenant	**Bass**; Don José's commander
Morales, a corporal	**Baritone**; guilty of sexual harassment towards Micaela
Frasquita, a gypsy girl	**Soprano**; Carmen's friend
Mercedes, a gypsy girl	**Soprano**; Carmen's friend
Dancairo, chief of the smugglers	**Tenor/baritone**
Remendado, smuggler	**Tenor**
Lillas Pastia, café proprietor	
Andres, an officer	

Plot structure and summary

Structure

Carmen is an opera in three acts with two scenes in the last act. The running time is approximately 2 hours 40 minutes.

Summary

The opera is set in early nineteenth-century Seville outside the entrance to a cigarette factory. An army barracks is opposite to the factory.

A young country girl, Micaëla is looking for one of the soldiers, Don José. She has a letter from his mother, who is trying to bring the young couple together. It seems likely that the mother's wish will be granted, up to the moment when Carmen, a gypsy worker from the cigarette factory arrives on the scene. She tosses a flower towards Don José, as if daring him to take up her challenge.

Shortly afterwards Carmen is involved in a fight with a fellow worker and Don José is ordered to escort her to jail, but she persuades him to allow her to escape.

In Lillas Pastia's café, Carmen flirts carelessly with the soldiers and her friends. She hears that Don José has just been released from detention after her escape and looks forward to meeting the man whom she mistakenly imagines to be as reckless as herself. Escamillo, the toreador, swaggers in and notices Carmen, who is cool towards him because she is waiting for Don José.

Don José does not live up to Carmen's expectation. She wants him to run away to the gypsy encampment with her, but he refuses to desert from the army.

She derides his dutiful attitude and, just then, his commanding officer arrives to order him back to barracks. Unable to tolerate a further humiliation, Don José draws his sword, a crime that forces him to take flight with Carmen.

At the gypsy encampment, Don José asks Carmen for forgiveness, but, realising that he is not the man she imagined him to be, Carmen rejects him.

Carmen and her two friends lay out cards and begin to tell their fortunes. The future looks bright for the two friends, but for Carmen the cards only show death.

Micaëla arrives at the camp to beg Don José to return home to see his mother who is dying. Escamillo also arrives back at the camp looking for Carmen. Sensing that he will soon be adding Carmen to his list of conquests, Escamillo invites everyone to his next bullfight.

After a jealous quarrel with Carmen, Don José agrees reluctantly to accompany Micaëla. As he leaves, he bitterly assures Carmen that they will meet again soon.

Carmen is at Escamillo's side before the bullfight, when a friend warns her that Don José is somewhere in the crowd. Carmen waits behind to confront him and flings at his feet the ring he gave her, telling him harshly that she despises him. As the crowd roars acclaim at Escamillo's victory over the bull, the heartbroken Don José draws a knife and stabs Carmen through the heart.

Listen out for . . .

If you are looking for a suggestion for the first opera to visit – this is it! Action packed from beginning to end, and full of stirring melodies and exciting rhythms.

Act One

Immediately	*Orchestra*	*Introduction* Instantly exciting and progressively informative as it introduces tunes and themes you will quickly come to associate with characters and events. Stark contrast between death theme and both happier and more exuberant moments.
5 mins	*Soldiers*	*Sur la place chacun passe* Low-key but catchy chorus.
10 mins	*Urchins*	*Avec la garde montante* Tuneful take-off of soldiers marching.
15 mins	*Factory girls*	*Dans l'air, nous suivons des yeux* Luscious, lazy chorus.
25 mins	*Carmen*	*L'amour est un oiseau rebelle (Habenera)* The *Habanera* is a little like a tango, only sexier.
30 mins	*Micaëla / Don José*	*Parle-moi de ma mère* Justifiably famous 'letter' duet.
45 mins	*Carmen*	*Tra la la la . . .* Insolent ripost from Carmen when she is accused of attacking another girl with a knife.
50 mins	*Carmen*, with occasional interjections from *Don José*	*Près des remparts de Séville (Seguidille)* The *Seguidilla* is a traditional Spanish dance. Carmen sings to entice Don José off the straight and narrow.

Act Two

Immediately	*Chorus*	*Gypsy dance* Full-blooded, party time at Lillas Pastia's hostelry.
2 mins	*Carmen* and *friends*	*Les tringles des sistres* Appreciative commentary on the dance.
10 mins	*Escamillo* and *Chorus*	*Votre toast, je peux vous le rendre* The Toreador song!

20 mins	Quintet between Carmen and her two gypsy friends and the smugglers	*Nous avons en tête une affaire* Plotting and planning . . .
25 mins	Carmen / Don José	*Je vais danser* Carmen attempts to seduce Don José with her dancing, but military bugles call him back to duty.
32 mins	Don José	*La fleur que tu m'avais jetée* The Flower Song. Glorious solo, reminding Carmen of the flower she had thrown to him.
37 mins	Carmen	*La-bas, la-bas dans la montagne* If you were half a man, you'd take me away from all this.
45 mins	Tutti	*Finale* A very French feel to 'Bel officier' at the beginning of this brilliant conclusion.

Act Three; Scene One

Immediately	Orchestra	*Prelude* Just when you thought there couldn't possibly be another wonderful melody . . .
10 mins	Carmen / Frasquita / Mercedes	*Melons! Coupons!* The ominous 'card' trio.
22 mins	Micaëla	*Je dis, que rien ne m'épouvante* A timidly melodious moment for sweet, innocent Micaëla.

Act Three; Scene Two

Immediately	Orchestra	*Entr'acte* Sets the swirling, bustling scene at the entrance to the bullring.
3 mins	Chorus	*A dos cuartos* Did this inspire Carl Orff?
10 mins	Carmen / Don José	*C'est toi* Final heart-wrenching duet.

Postscript

Carmen Jones, an updated version of *Carmen*, was created by Oscar
Hammerstein II and staged in New York in 1943. The cigarette factory is transformed into a parachute factory; Don José is Corporal Joe
and Cindy Lou replaces Micaela as his childhood sweetheart. With
perfect logic, Escamillo is reborn as the prize-fighter Husky Miller, for
whom, in this version, both ladies lust.

Although the orchestration remains remarkably true to Bizet's original design, the songs seem to translate automatically into this newer
and more topical version. Husky Miller's party piece, *Stan' up and
fight*, is every bit as appropriate to his character, as its alter ego, the
Toreador's song is for Escamillo in *Carmen*. *Beat out dat rhythm on a
drum*, has words so perfectly suited to Bizet's music, that it could easily be mistaken for original composition, were it not for the blatantly
up-to-date message. In his reworking of the characters, rather than,
for the large part, the music, Oscar Hammerstein's interpretation
stands as a classic in its own right. There have been numerous
attempts over the years to take a fresh look at accepted works, but
none has ever managed to achieve the heights of inspiration that are
evident in *Carmen Jones*.

PROSPER MÉRIMÉE (1803–70)

The historian and writer, Prosper Mérimée wrote the novel
Carmen in his forties. This original version was even stronger
and more uncompromising than the libretto, compiled for Bizet
by Meilhac and Halévy. In Mérimée's story, Don José's
account of his downfall at the hands of a woman, suggests the
lustful infatuation of a tough guy, rather than the wretched
longings of a lovesick loon.

Recommended recordings

There have been some luscious Carmens, but Don José must also sing
to thrill. Of the various partnerships available on disc, it would be the
Don José of José Carreras that tipped the balance for me. Therefore it
has to be the Deutsche Grammophon digital recording with Herbert
von Karajan conducting the Berlin Philharmonic and Agnes Baltsa in
the role of Carmen.

If you enjoyed this, now try . . .

What about *Carmen Jones*, the superb realisation of Bizet's opera by Oscar Hammerstein II. The film soundtrack recording has the strongest imaginable cast, with Marilyn Horne as Carmen Jones, LeVern Hutcherson as Corporal Joe, Marvin Hayes as Husky Miller and the inimitable Pearl Bailey as Frankie. This work enjoys well-deserved success and stands as a creative masterpiece in its own right.

GIACOMO PUCCINI
(1858–1924)

Puccini was immersed in music from birth and was the fifth generation of Puccini musicians and composers to serve the town of Lucca in Italy. By the age of 14 he was playing the organ at San Martino and San Michele, as well as in numerous other local churches.

At the age of 18 he attended a performance of Verdi's *Aida*, and this made such an impression on the young musician that he was determined to become a composer of operas. In 1880, thanks to the financial support of his uncle, another musician, Puccini was able to accept a place at the music conservatory in Milan. An opera, *Le villi*, written during his time as a student failed to win the conservatory's prize, but was taken up by Giulio Ricordi. Not only did this mark the beginning of a notable career for Puccini, but also began his lifelong association with the publishing house, Ricordi.

Puccini's first big success came with the opera, *Manon Lescaut* and he was to use the same two librettists, the poet Giuseppe Giacosa and the literary pragmatist Luigi Illica for his next opera, *La Bohème*.

Puccini's particular gifts lay in his innate sense of theatre and in his ability to write a really good and memorable tune. With negligible padding and evocative musical images, his scores move swiftly, effortlessly carrying the audience along.

Tragically, this eminent promoter of the voice died from a heart attack resulting from cancer of the larynx at the age of 65, leaving his final opera, *Turandot*, to be finished by the Italian composer Franco Alfano (1875–1954). All Italy mourned Puccini's death, the man many revered as the only true successor of Giuseppe Verdi.

La Bohème

Background information

The composers Giacomo Puccini and Ruggero Leoncavallo had been friends right up to the moment of a fateful meeting in a café in Milan in 1893. Both were beginning to enjoy the fruits of success, Puccini with his opera *Manon Lescaut* and Leoncavallo with his opera *I Pagliacci*. As the conversation turned to each composer's next project, it became apparent that both men intended to set a libretto from the same source. A new opera, *La Bohème*, was to be based on Henry Murger's work, *Scènes de la vie de Bohème*. Leoncavallo's case was that he had already offered the libretto to Puccini, who had refused it, prompting Leoncavallo to take up the project himself.

It seems that Puccini must have changed his mind, for his version was also well under way by this time. Whatever the rights and wrongs of the situation, the two men would remain implacable enemies for the rest of their lives.

Time and public taste have proved Puccini's *La Bohème* the victor, possibly because it is the best possible vehicle for this composer's facility for writing extraordinary music to arouse an audience's empathy with the 'ordinary' characters who people this work.

Characters

Marcello, a painter	**Baritone**; Rodolfo's garret-mate; wins Musetta's heart
Rodolfo, a poet	**Tenor**; male romantic lead
Colline, a philosopher	**Bass**; Young and poor like his garret-mates, Rudolfo and Marcello
Schaunard, a musician	**Baritone**; fourth garret-mate
Benoit, the landlord	**Bass**; elderly; easily distracted by drink
Mimi, an embroideress	**Soprano**; female romantic lead
Musetta, a free spirit	**Soprano**; feisty show-off
Alcindoro, a state councillor	**Tenor**; initially, Musetta's protector
Parpignal, the toy seller	
Customers officer	
Customs sergeant	

Plot structure and summary

Structure

La Bohème is a verismo opera in four acts and has a running time of approximately 1 hour 45 minutes.

Summary

Inside the garret of four bohemians on Christmas Eve, Rudolfo and Marcello are trying to work, but are so cold they are forced to burn an old movie script on the fire. First Colline and then Schaunard join them. The latter has brought more food than they can imagine as he has been well paid for his latest work. Benoit arrives demanding the rent, but the four men ply him with drink and the old fool soon forgets why he is there.

The friends decide to visit the Café Momus and Rudolfo arranges to meet them once he has finished his latest script. Mimi knocks at the door seeking a light for her candle and before Rudolfo can light a match, the two are deeply in love.

In the Latin Quarter of Paris Musetta, an ex-girlfriend of Marcello, is behaving badly towards her new protector, Alcindoro. Sending him off on an errand, she makes a play for Marcello. Alcindoro returns to find that Musetta has left Café Momus with Marcello, leaving Alcindoro to pay both bills.

The bohemians' lifestyle has begun to take its toll. There are many quarrels now between the two couples and even Rudolfo and Mimi talk of splitting up. Mimi's health has deteriorated which persuades Rudolfo and herself to stay together until the spring.

Some time later, Marcello and Rudolfo are found consoling each other, for both girls have found other admirers. The discussion turns into rowdy horseplay, which Musetta interrupts. She has come to tell the friends that Mimi is alone and dying from tuberculosis. Rudolfo brings Mimi home where, surrounded by her friends and lover, she dies.

Listen our for . . .

Act One

18 mins	*Rudolfo*	*Che gelida manina* Your tiny hand is frozen, scarcely requires an introduction, and leads into . . .
25 mins	*Mimi*	*Si. Mi chamano Mimi* Having heard all about Rudolfo, Mimi reveals a little about herself.
30 mins	*Rudolfo / Mimi*	*O soave fanciulla,* Sensational love duet.

Act Two

Immediately	*Tutti*	Glorious hullabaloo of the street vendors and customers outside Café Momus
10 mins	*Musetta*	*Quando m'en vo* Naughty Musetta's Waltz Song.
18 mins	*Tutti*	*Finale; La Ritirata* 'The Tattoo'. A band approaches; Musetta lands poor Alcindoro with the bill and exits with the friends.

Act Three

Immediately	*Orchestra, chorus*	Atmospheric opening to an act heavy with disillusionment and impending tragedy.
6 mins	*Mimi / Marcello*	*O buon Marcello, aiuto, aiuto!* 'Please help me, Marcello!' Mimi is in despair because of Rudolfo's jealousy.
20 mins	*Mimi*	*Donde lieta uscì al tuo grido* Mimi finds the courage to finish the relationship with Rudolfo. Maybe the music is just too beautiful, for they postpone their parting until the spring.

Act Four

20 mins	*Mimi / Rudolfo*	*Sono andati?* The final love duet. 'Are we alone?' Mimi wants the friends to leave so that she can be alone with Rudolfo to tell him how much she loves him.
30 mins	*Rudolfo / Marcello / Musetta / Schaundard / Colline*	*Che ha detto il medico?* 'What did the doctor say?' Mimi's death scene.

Postscript

The opening night of *La Bohème* was held at the Teatro Regio in Turin, with Toscanini conducting. The audience identified immediately with the four lovable rogues and the tragic heroine, although the conversational style of some of the singing was a new and unexpected turn of events. The music critics, however, were merciless in their condemnation. Complaints that this work could not be compared with the earlier *Manon Lescaut*, and that Puccini should get back to some serious work, were perhaps a measure of the ease with which *La Bohème* fastened itself on the ear and charmed the audience. For the critics to accept a new work, it would perhaps have needed some elements of musical exclusivity that only they could appreciate, and the virtue of *La Bohème* is that its simple, fast-moving plot and memorable tunes are instantly accessible to everyone.

Because *La Bohème* is an opera in the traditional sense, it is easy to imagine that Puccini lived and composed long before he did, but you will hear some orchestral playing that could have come straight from the soundtrack of a Hollywood movie. This composer's ability to elicit an emotional response from almost any audience cannot have been lost on those early movie makers and the 'Puccini' style was frequently employed as a mood enhancer.

Rooted in the traditions of the past, but with an acute awareness of contemporary preferences and an uncanny sense of theatre, Puccini's music has a timeless quality that ensures it will never fall victim to changing fashions.

Recommended recordings

There are some outstanding recordings of this opera. Just how do you choose between Jussi Björling and Luciano Pavarotti in the role of Rudolfo? Björling sings on the earlier EMI mono recording and Pavarotti on Decca. Once again, it seems that we are still waiting for today's singers to form a real challenge to these landmark recordings. In the end it has to be Pavarotti, who surpasses every expectation you might have. Mirella Freni is his Mimi, Elizabeth Harwood plays Musetta and Herbert von Karajan conducts the Berlin Philharmonic Orchestra.

If you enoyed this, now try . . .

Madame Butterfly has pathos, melody and the *humming chorus*; *Tosca* can have Maria Callas at her scintillating best, together with a radiant Giuseppe di Stefano as Cavaradossi and the powerful characterisation of Tito Gobbi in the role of Scarpia, if you choose the EMI classics recording. *Turandot* is stunning and *Gianni Schicchi* has 'O my beloved father'. And that's just the beginning. Puccini produced such a wealth of operatic music, you can't go wrong.

GEORGE GERSHWIN
(1898–1937)

Born in Brooklyn, USA, through his compositions George Gershwin proved himself the consummate entertainer. He could be described as Jack of all trades . . . and master of them all! His greatest gift was his ability to create music that crossed the divide between so-called classical and popular, allowing him to appeal to an audience on many different levels.

Absorbing folk idioms in America was, and is, a richly rewarding quest, since the traditions of so many cultures are represented in one country. George Gershwin took full advantage of both these and music's classical heritage, lacing his evocative 'classical' compositions with the rhythms and tonal exuberance of Jazz, and bringing expansive Romantic themes and structure into his hits for Tin Pan Alley and Broadway.

As a young man keenly attuned to his times, he wrote hits for Tin Pan Alley, and by the 1920s had become the most successful composer of musicals on Broadway. His brother, Ira, wrote most of the lyrics and proved himself to be as inspired a craftsman with words as was George with music.

In 1924, Gershwin moved into a new sphere of music with his composition for piano and Paul Whiteman's Jazz orchestra, *Rhapsody in Blue*. This cemented his position as a leading composer of American music and prompted him to include more 'serious' works in his vast catalogue of compositions.

As well as numerous songs and musicals, Gershwin produced a Piano Concerto in 1925 and the orchestral tone poem *An American in Paris* in 1928. More musicals followed and in 1935, his American Folk opera, *Porgy and Bess*, with a libretto by DuBose Heyward and George's brother Ira Gershwin, premiered in New York, following a preview in Boston.

Such an amalgam of styles had never before been presented to a public thoroughly familiar with Gershwin's sometimes sentimental, always catchy melodies.

An evening with Gershwin could always be guaranteed to leave an audience with a song in the heart and a smile on the lips, but *Porgy and Bess* delved far deeper into social issues and demanded the formulation of quite a different response. Despite providing some of the most enduring melodies to have emanated from any opera, *Porgy and Bess* was not received with unconditional acclaim, seeming pretentious to some and patronising to others. Fortunately, time and changing attitudes have allowed this work to enjoy the level of success it merits.

It is entirely likely that George Gershwin employed someone else to prepare orchestral scores, although credit for any piano score or musical theme was certainly his. Following *Porgy and Bess*, he devoted himself almost entirely to Hollywood and the new craft of film scores. George Gershwin died in Beverly Hills from the effects of a brain tumour, just before his fortieth birthday. He left behind a legacy of incalculable value not just to his fellow Americans, but to music lovers everywhere.

Porgy and Bess

Background information

DuBose Heyward's original story had been inspired by a newspaper article concerning a disabled black American who had murdered a woman. 'Goat Sammy' had then tried to evade capture by escaping from the police in his goat cart.

Heyward's evocative tale breathed life into the vividly drawn characters who inhabited Catfish Row and captured the imagination of

George Gershwin, who was searching for a subject upon which to base his first full-length opera.

The finished piece has been subject to a number of revisions, including the removal of the sung recitative. This was replaced by dialogue, but *Porgy and Bess* is an opera, not a play with songs, and this sort of meddling diminishes Gershwin's original work.

Each decade has seen a fresh surge of appreciation for *Porgy and Bess* and in the 1980s the opera gained mainstream acceptance, when it was staged both in Houston and at the Met'. In the 1990s, first Glyndebourne and then Covent Garden staged *Porgy and Bess*, reinforcing its position as an opera worthy of inclusion in the twentieth-century repertoire of any leading house.

Characters

Porgy, a disabled man — **Bass-baritone**; male lead; falls in love with Bess

Bess, a free spirit — **Soprano**; female lead

Crown, a stevedore — **Baritone**; Bess's lover; brawler, murderer and eventual murder victim

Sportin' Life, a drug dealer — **Tenor**; another of Bess's admirers and one who has more than love to offer

Robbins, 'crap' game player — **Tenor**; Crown's victim

Serena, Robbin's wife — **Soprano**; disapproves of Bess

Jake, a fisherman — **Baritone**; a fisher of souls . . . ? Sadly, he drowns.

Clara, Jake's wife — **Soprano**; caring and sharing

Maria, shop owner — **Contralto**; formidably respectable

Jasbo Brown, Jazz pianist

Scipio, a local boy

Frazier, amateur con-man and would-be lawyer

Mr Archdale, wealthy white man

Other characters from 'Catfish Row' include *Jim, Peter, Lily* and *Nelson*.

Plot structure and summary

Structure

Porgy and Bess is a 'Folk' opera in three acts; two scenes in Act One, four scenes in Act Two and three scenes in Act Three. The running time is approximately 3 hours and 15 minutes

Summary

Evening in Catfish Row, and the men have gathered for a crap game. Crown loses and kills Robbins in his fury. The crowd disperses, leaving Serena to grieve over her husband's body, and Bess, who slips away through the only open door . . . the door to Porgy's house. Porgy and Bess fall in love and gradually, thanks to Porgy's good name, Bess becomes accepted by the rest of the community.

Everyone is leaving for a picnic and Porgy has persuaded Bess to go without him. Seeing her alone, Crown, who has been in hiding since the murder, calls her over and Bess is lured away. When Bess is brought home to Porgy after two days in the woods, she is delirious and has to be confined to bed for a week. Once she recovers, Bess confesses everything and says that she wants to stay with Porgy.

A terrible storm blows up. Jake has gone fishing, and Crown arrives searching for Bess, who refuses to leave with him. In a jealous rage, Crown threatens to kill Porgy. Jake's wife, Clara, hands her baby daughter to Bess and rushes out into the storm to search for her husband.

When the storm passes, it becomes clear that both Jake and Clara are dead. At first, it seems that Crown too has been killed, but Crown plans to kill Porgy. Porgy sees him coming and strikes the first blow, killing Crown.

When the police arrive to investigate Crown's death, they inform Porgy that he will be required to identify the body. Taunted by Sportin' Life, Porgy refuses and is dragged away by the police. Sportin' Life convinces Bess that she must leave with him and begin a new life in New York. Confused and distraught, Bess agrees.

Having established that the killing was done in self-defence, Porgy returns home after a week. He has gifts for all his friends as he won money at crap games whilst in jail. When he discovers that Bess has gone to New York with Sportin' Life, he resolves to bring her back.

Listen out for . . .

Act One; Scene One

Immediately	*Orchestra*	Dynamic opening and the Jazz piano of *Jasbo Brown*.
5 mins	*Clara*	*Summertime* Clara's glorious lullaby is a languid, heat-hazed interlude before the crap game.
15 mins	*Jake/Chorus*	*A woman is a sometime thing* Catchy, cynical view of womankind.

Act One; Scene Two

50 mins	*Serena*	*My man's gone now* Quintessential grieving song.
55 mins	*Bess/Chorus*	*Oh, the train is at the station* Strong finale to the act, reminiscent of black-and-white film musical, but with more demanding vocal line.

Act Two; Scene One

Immediately	*Jake/Chorus*	*It take a long pull to get there* Work song.
5 mins	*Porgy*	*I got plenty of nuttin'* Memorable, stirring; simply brilliant.
10 mins	*Maria*	*I hates yo' struttin' style* Everyone's opinion of Sportin' Life, expressed with the utmost clarity.
25 mins	*Porgy/Bess*	*Bess you is my woman now* Sumptuously melodic; poignant and uplifting.

Act Two; Scene Two

40 mins	*Sportin' Life*	*It ain't necessarily so* Catchy music and inspired lyrics; no wonder this naughty number became a worldwide favourite.

Act Two; Scene Three

65 mins	*Chorus*	*Oh dey's so fresh an' fine* A refreshing and evocative interlude after the turgid drama stirred up by Bess and Crown.
75 mins	*Porgy/Bess*	*I wants to stay here* Touching duet.

Act Two; Scene Four

85 mins	*Chorus*	*Oh, Doctor Jesus, look down on me wi' pity* Atmospheric storm scene, six solo voices offer up prayers and the confusion is abated.
90 mins	*Tutti*	*Oh, dere's somebody knockin' at the door* Catchy tune that belies the character of the 'knocker'.
100 mins	*Crown*	*A red-headed woman* Foot-tapping piece of bragging for Crown.

Act Three; Scene One

2 mins	*Chorus*	*Clara, Clara, don't you be downhearted* Peaceful chorus after the storm.
10 mins	*Bess*	*Summertime* Luckily Bess is left holding the baby, so the most beautiful lullaby ever written gets a second airing.

Act Three; Scene Two

| 15 mins | *Sportin' Life* | *There's a boat dat's leavin' soon for New York* |
| | | Brilliantly crafted, crafty solo, with stunning orchestral climax to the scene. |

Act Three; Scene Three

20 mins	*Orchestral / Tutti*	*Good mornin' sistuh!*
		Big symphonic opening, leading to feel-good scene and welcome home for Porgy.
On to the end of the opera . . .		Every moment draws up a thread of the story and leads to the inevitably powerful conclusion.

Postscript

DuBose (Edwin) Heyward (1885–1940)

This writer's work centered predominantly upon the lives of poor, black families in the southern states of the United States. His first novel, *Porgy*, published in 1925, was set on the waterfront at Charleston, South Carolina, and amongst other elements was noteworthy because it introduced the local black 'Gulleh' dialect to a wider audience.

Heyward wrote another five novels, collaborating with his wife Dorothy Heyward in the dramatisation of two of these, *Porgy* and *Mamba's Daughter*.

Gershwin approached Heyward with a view to creating opera based on *Porgy*, but the Heyward's dramatisation was to be staged by the New York Theatre Guild. After the success of this production, Gershwin tried again and now Heyward agreed to collaborate with Ira Gershwin in the preparation of a libretto.

Recommended recordings

Simon Rattle conducting the London Philharmonic recreates the taut, electrifying experience of *Porgy and Bess* at Glyndebourne. With Willard White as Porgy, Cynthia Harmon as Bess, Damon Evans as Sportin' Life and a vibrant supporting cast, this three-disc collection from EMI digital is a 'must have' for any music lover.

This is one opera where the individual songs are so strong, you may want to add a 'highlights' album to your collection.

If you've enjoyed this, now try

The world really is your oyster now, for Gershwin wrote music for every age and every mood, enriched by a multitude of styles. You could shoot off in any one of a dozen different musical directions and find some Gershwin to enjoy. The musical *Crazy for You,* based on the 1930s show *Girl Crazy*, proved the enduring quality of George Gershwin's melodies, when it opened to rave revues on Broadway in 1992, and in the West End the following year.

And now try

It would be impossible to mention every wonderful tune from the world of opera, but here are 20 more of my favourites for you to enjoy.

Aria	Opera	Composer
'Ah! non giunge'	*La Sonnambula*	Vincenzo Bellini
'Alma del core'	*La costanza in amor*	Antonio Caldara
'Bell Song, The'	*Lakme*	Leo Delibes
'Caro nome che il mio cor'	*Rigoletto*	Guiseppe Verdi
'Casta Diva'	*Norma*	Vincenzo Bellini
'Che faro senza Euridice'	*Orfeo ed Euridice*	Christoph W. Gluck
'Easter Hymn'	*Cavalleria rusticana*	Pietro Mascagni
'Elsa's dream'	*Lohengrin*	Richard Wagner
'Hark! The echoing air'	*The Fairy Queen*	Henry Purcell
'In questa reggia'	*Turandot*	Giacomo Puccini
'La mamma morta'	*Andrea Chenier*	Umberto Giordano
'Madamina'	*Don Giovanni*	W. Amadeus Mozart
'O del mio dolce ardor'	*Elena e Paride*	Christoph W. Gluck
'Oh mio bambino caro'	*Gianni Schicci*	Giacomo Puccini

'Ombra mai fu'	*Xerxes*	George Handel
'Pearl Fisher's duet, The'	*Les Pêcheurs de perles*	Georges Bizet
'Softly awakes my heart'	*Samson and Delilah*	Camille Saint-Saëns
'Stizzoso, mio stizzoso'	*La serva padrona*	Giovanni B. Pergolesi
'Una furtiva lagrima'	*L'elisir d'amore*	Gaetano Donizetti
'Vissi d'arte'	*Tosca*	Giacomo Puccini

If you have enjoyed the classical style of singing, but don't always feel in the mood for opera, there are other types of vocal music for you to explore; here are a few.

Oratorio

A musical performance with a religious theme intended for a concert setting, involving chorus, soloists and orchestra, or other musical accompaniment.

Suggestions

Handel's *Messiah* and *Judas Maccabeus*; Mendelssohn's *Elijah*; Bach's *Christmas Oratorio*; Haydn's *Creation*; Berlioz' *The Childhood of Christ*; Elgar's *The Dream of Gerontius*; Michael Tippett's *A Child of our Time*; Benjamin Britten', *War Requiem*.

Requiem

A Mass for the dead. Don't be put off since these works contain some of the most beautiful music every written.

Suggestions

Requiems by Mozart, Berlioz, Verdi, Brahms and Fauré.

Operetta

Light opera, musical comedy.

Suggestions

The Merry Widow by Franz Lehar; *Orpheus in the Underworld* by Jacques Offenbach; *Die Fledermaus* by Johann Strauss; *HMS*

Pinafore by Gilbert and Sullivan; *Show Boat* by Jerome Kern; *Oklahoma* by Rodgers and Hammerstein; *My Fair Lady* by Lerner and Loewe; *West Side Story* with music by Leonard Bernstein and lyrics by Stephen Sondheim; *Fiddler on the Roof* with music by Jerry Bock and lyrics by Sheldon Harnick; *Oliver!* by Lionel Bart; *Sunset Boulevard* by Andrew Lloyd Webber; *Les Misérables* by Boublil and Schoenberg.

Early Music

Here is a tiny selection of available CDs: *The English Orpheus*, Emma Kirkby (soprano) and Anthony Rooley (lute and orpharion), performing the music of John Dowland 1562–1626; *Baroque Duet*, Kathleen Battle (soprano), Wynton Marsalis (trumpet); *Henry Purcell Songs and Airs*, Emma Kirkby (soprano). And for a complete wind-down with some very early music: *A feather on the breath of God*, sequences and hymns by Hildegard of Bingen, 1098–1179.

Lieder

This term is used to describe the type of Romantic Art song written by composers such as Schubert, Schumann, Brahms, Strauss and Wolf. Usually sung to a piano accompaniment, the songs generally tell a story and are full of character. Schubert is an excellent composer with whom to begin your investigations into this style. Songs such as *The Trout*, which you can also enjoy in a quintet version for instruments, are full of humour and memorable tunes; works such as the song cycle *Die schöne müllerin* (The Beautiful Maid of the Mill), or the piece for piano, clarinet and voice, *The Shepherd on the Rock*, are also melodious and dramatic. If you enjoy these suggestions, Schubert wrote over 600 songs, so there are plenty more to try before you need to start on another composer!

GLOSSARY

argomento It. plot summary
aria a solo song
arietta a shorter solo song
arpeggio the notes of a chord sounding one after the other rather than together
atonal music that is not in 'key'

ballad a simple song; sometimes each verse is sung to the same tune
ballad opera a type of musical play popular in England in the eighteenth and nineteenth centuries (see John Gay, *A Beggar's Opera* p.67)
bar the term used to describe the subdivision of written music into units
barcarolle a boating song of the gently swing and glide type
bel canto (lit. beautiful singing) the classical style of singing which originated in Italy in the seventeenth century; characterised by effortless technique and beautiful tone
Brindisi drinking song
brio vigour
buffa comic (see *opera buffa*)

cabaletta the climax of some arias; fast and showy
cadenza a florid and brilliant passage, usually for the solo performer and generally placed at the end of a piece. Some may be improvised by the individual, others are written out
canon two or more voices, or instruments, winding tunes around each other

cantata lit. sung music

canzone a song that appears in its own right as it would in a play

castrato a male singer who has been castrated in order to retain an unbroken voice

cavatina a short aria-type composition

chorale a hymn-like piece

claque group of paid supporters

coda (lit. tail) an added section, placed at the end of a composition, to make a good finish

colla voce with the voice

coloratura (lit. coloured) a technically expert voice, capable of complex and florid movement

comic opera used as a translation for various national comic styles, or to describe operas such as those written by Gilbert and Sullivan

comique see **opera comique**

continuo keyboard accompaniment that underpins the music

contrapuntal music consisting of two or more strands heard simultaneously

cor anglais (lit. English horn) actually a deep-toned member of the oboe family; listen out for this instrument in Wagner

counterpoint effective combination of two simultaneous musical lines

crescendo getting louder

cross rhythms two or more groups of instruments playing together, each using a different rhythm, or a number of beats in a bar

Czardas a Hungarian gypsy dance

da capo (lit. from the top) from the beginning

descant a high-pitched line adding some embellishment above the tune

desk a music stand for two

diminuendo gradually becoming softer

discord two or more notes played together that do not sound harmonious

Diva a term of respect used to denote outstanding female performers

divertissement a diversion, possibly a dance

duet a composition for two voices

Ecossaise a Scottish dance

ENO English National Opera Company

ensemble (lit. together) more than four people playing or singing together

entr'acte a piece of music played between two acts

falsetto high, unbroken sounding notes, made by a male with a mature, broken voice
figure a snatch of music, complete in itself
finale the end piece of music
forte loud
fortissimo extremely loud

Gavotte a stately dance
glee a simple English song
glissando a sliding effect, up or down a series of notes
Grand Opera not a term much in use today, it refers to the more elaborate form of opera, *grandeur, large forces, ballet*, etc, of the type that flourished in France from the early nineteenth century, into the twentieth

Intendant the administrator of the opera house
interlude see **entr'acte**
Intermezzo lit. in the middle
interval the distance between two notes, or the time between two acts
intonation the pitch of a note

key the note around which a musical passage gravitates; to sing 'off key' means 'out of tune'; a key is also one of the series of visible levers on a keyboard instrument
key signature musical symbols, sharps or flats, which appear at the beginning of a piece of written music, indicating the key of the music

Leitmotif a snatch of music associated with a character, a mood, or an idea
light opera as the name suggests, and possibly containing some spoken dialogue; often referred to as operetta

madrigal a contrapuntal composition for voices; sometimes unaccompanied
Maestro (lit. master) a term of respect used to denote outstanding male performers
major a reference to the key of the music; a major key is thought to create a happier sound world than the 'melancholy' minor key
masque an early dramatic production combining poetry, music and dancing
Mazurka a Polish dance

melodrama sometimes referred to in the French style, *melodrame*; a recitation to music

melodramma dramatic text written to be set to music; *melodramma seria* is therefore the same as *opera seria*

metastasian a reference to the famous Italian librettist and poet, Metastasio

minuet a stately dance

modal, modes an earlier system of music than the key arrangement most commonly used today

modulation a change of key

motet a sacred choral composition, usually unaccompanied

musical a modern dramatic musical production, may contain some dialogue

Music Director a major force in decision making and training for all musical matters; may also take prominent role as conductor

mute something which damps down the sound of an instrument

obbligato a light accompaniment; something which may not be left out

octave the same note played eight notes higher, or lower

octet a piece for eight people

opera buffa comic opera

opera comique French opera with spoken words; not exclusively comic style

opera seria serious opera

oratorio a biblical work for singers and orchestra, usually intended for concert, rather than stage performance

orchestration written music for the orchestra

overture an orchestral introduction

Parlante, parlando (lit. speaking) sung in a style that imitates the natural inflections of speech

patter song song with fast-moving words

pedal a sustained note in the bass; a lever at the bass of a piano, etc. used to sustain notes

piano soft

pianissimo very soft

prestissimo as fast as possible

presto very fast

Prima Donna lit. first lady

Producer the person responsible for putting on an opera

Prologue a sung piece before 'curtain up'

quasi as if, almost, like

recitative a type of vocal writing that follows the natural rhythms of speech

Repetiteur usually a pianist, this person is responsible for coaching singers in their roles

reprise repeat

requiem a mass for the dead, set to music

rhapsody romantic musical piece in free form

ritornello a short, recurring passage for orchestra

romanza a sentimental solo song

rubato the rhythm of a piece is stretched and broadened

scale a sequence of notes in ascending, or descending pitch

scherzo lit. a joke

score the complete written-out music, showing every part to be played or sung

segue carrying straight on; seamless joining of two musical sections

serenade love songs performed 'out of doors', usually in the evening; orchestral serenades also exist; generally reflecting a relaxed 'evening' style

seria see **opera seria**

serialism the ordering of music according to a fixed plan

sforzando suddenly loud

Siciliana an early aria-type composition with simple harmonies and lifting rhythms, associated with pastoral scenes; sometimes melancholy

Singspiel an opera with spoken dialogue between songs

sonority to do with the quality and depth of sound

sotto voce (lit. under the voice) soft, or murmured singing

soubrette a light-hearted soprano role, often a maid

Sprechgesang speaking in a prescribed pitch

staccato short and detached

stave five horizontal lines drawn across a page upon which musical notes are written

strings instruments of the string family

tempo time; speed

tessitura the most consistent range of pitch of a piece

transposition the rewriting of a piece of music in a higher or lower key

treble a child's voice in the soprano range

trill two alternating notes sung repeatedly and quickly
triplet three notes to be played or sung in the time of two
tutti all together

unison all voices singing the same line

verismo true to life
vibrato vibrating; in the worst cases, this emotion-promoting tool becomes a wobble
vivace quick and lively
voce voice

BIBLIOGRAPHY

Carr, Francis,
Mozart and Constanze,
John Murray, 1983

Greenfield, Edward, March, Ivan,
and Layton, Robert,
*The Penguin Guide to Opera on
Compact Discs,*
Penguin, 1993

Harman, Alec, and Milner, Anthony,
Late Renaissance and Baroque Music,
Barry and Jenkins, 1962

Hines, Jerome
Great Singers on Great Singing,
St Edmundsbury Press
Ltd, 1982

Jablonski, Edward, and Stewart,
Lawrence D.,
The Gershwin Years,
New York, Da Capo Press,
1996

Osborne, Charles,
Verdi; A Life in the Theatre,
Micheal O'Mara Books
Ltd, 1987

Till, Nicholas,
Rossini,
Omnibus, 1983

Weiss, Pietro, and Taruskin, Richard,
*Music in the Western World;
A History in Documents,*
Macmillian, 1984

INDEX